End papers. Diarama of a battle scene depicting the Polish Lancers of the Guard in 30 cm and 15 cm figures made in a latex composition. Here only the simplest of materials is used to make the diarama— sand. The placing of different size models creates the illusion of distance.

MAKING
MODEL SOLDIERS
OF THE WORLD

MAKING

MODEL SOLDIERS

OF THE WORLD

JACK CASSIN-SCOTT

STEPHEN HOPE BOOKS
LONDON

First published in Great Britain 1973 by
Stephen Hope Books Limited
47 Whitehall, London, SW1A 2BX

ISBN 0 903792 01

Additional information by
PENELOPE FABB
Photography by
JACK BLAKE

Typeset and printed in Great Britain by
the Hope Burgess Group, on
High Speed Blade Coated Cartridge 118GSM
Bound by James Burn Ltd. Esher

Contents

List of Colour Plates

French Grenadier
in parade dress 1806-14

List of Black and White Plates

To my son Tony

Preface

The making of model soldiers for the beginner must seem to be an almost impossible task. Any attempt to copy the production methods of manufacturers is far beyond the enthusiast. Many of the techniques explained must, by the mere conditions imposed, fall into the unorthodox category. Bearing in mind that the average model soldier enthusiast's studio is nothing more than the kitchen or dining room table with a limited space, I offer the first steps in the making of model soldiers.

Perhaps the beginner will accuse me of being too technical, I hope not, but nonetheless I hope he or she will understand the great problems in trying to simplify what is after all a difficult form of art with a great deal of labour involved, and no labour, even of love, is without its problems.

It is impossible to thank everyone for their kind help and advice, nor all the individual makers of the superb models which appear throughout the coloured plates in this book and the many that are not mentioned who directly or indirectly made this book possible.

My special thanks must go to John and Penelope Fabb and Melvin Coles for allowing me permission to have photographs taken of part of their model soldier collections, and to Penny again, for her painting and assembling of many of the figures.

I have tried to keep both tools and materials down to a minimum and have given only the basic simple instructions without, I hope, minimising that practice and more practice is the only way to achieve the ultimo—that of creating at least one of your very own models, in this fascinating hobby of model soldier making.

Jack Cassin-Scott   *London* 1973

A 30 cm latex composition figure of a British paratrooper (Red Beret) of the post World War II period is seen here carrying the F.N. rifle. This regiment won fame for their exploits in World War II.

Introduction

Within the limits of this volume there is just one basic idea—that of showing a way towards the satisfying hobby of making model soldiers. So from the past we find pleasure for the future. There are no rigid rules as to the type of materials used or any fixed notions on the methods or techniques.

The model solider shows the splendour of the military uniforms which have always been a great attraction throughout the ages both to the soldier himself and the onlooker. The models of the Napoleonic era bring back the vivid images of the Grand Army with its many different uniforms worn with such distinction by so many nations on a variety of battle fronts. They are all representative of their countries but fascinatingly diverse in character. Famous battles, whose names made history, live on through the model soldier, retaining the excitement of the flashing sabre, the charging horseman, the noise and smoke from the roaring cannons.

Our model soldiers show the changing styles of uniforms, their complexity and character and show further that the rule of an ambitious Frenchman, Napoleon Bonaparte, influenced the uniform fashion of nearly all the world for many decades.

The Hungarian Hussars were to find their counterpart in every country in Europe and eventually found their way to the Americas. The czapka headdress and the kurtka tunic of the Polish Volunteers were copied by Lancers throughout Europe. Great Britain and Russia were alone in their field of individual design of military uniform, but after the catastrophic Russian campaign of 1812 the Russian type Cossack national costume influenced many European military modes, especially the German States. The Highland troops of Scotland serving in the British army followed their own fashion and did not have any imitators, except perhaps the Greeks whose kilts had their own history and tradition.

Model soldiers have become a new and exciting way of life, both in their collecting and making. Thousands of model soldier collectors show a great reluctance in producing their own models because of what appears to be a formidable task to produce such an intricate and finely detailed figure. Many have tried converting and have created original pieces from existing manufactured models; the effort has been well worth while. Whilst discussing conversions, the main purpose of this book is to show the way to produce a model in a simple straightforward modelling technique from the basic form into a material of one's own choosing, whichever best serves the individual purpose. We can adapt modern materials which science has developed to form new ideas and ways in producing our model soldiers. Such materials as Polyester Resins, Silicone Rubbers, Latex, Vinamold Compounds, Liquid Plastics and many more tend to extend the horizon of the model soldier student enthusiast beyond the simple conversion stage. These materials, combined with the new modelling compounds now available, make a new step forward to producing original models. There are two methods of achieving our ultimate result, these are either by modelling or by sculpture. Modelling is a process of placing on, or building up, whilst sculpture is a cutting away from either wood or a solid mass of material. The technique of sculpture is full of pitfalls for the unwary and the inexperienced, one false cut with the knife or chisel and the aspiration of the moment is ruined. As one must begin somewhere, modelling is, with a few simple rules, compared with sculpture, the most satisfying method for the beginner. The placing on and the taking off can be made without any drastic surgical operation if any mistake has been made.

As previously stated the fundamental reason for this book is to show the enthusiast who has no experience in the art of modelling, a way or technique to overcome the first hurdles of this fascinating hobby of model soldier making. Before commencing remember one thing, that the technique described must not be regarded as the only method, there are many methods and techniques and all should be tried at one time or another. This way you will create your own workable method.

The work of the amateur model maker becomes twofold, not only must the study of serious historical research be intensified but a further study of books on the anatomy of people and animals must be included in the search for knowledge. Study the world around you and you will be surprised how much one can learn by taking a keen interest in statues and paintings. Don't get discouraged, the effort will be well worth while. The principles of model-making follow a fairly set pattern, first the preliminary modelled figure, then the mould and finally the finished model in the composition of one's choice, the ways and means are described in the following pages.

The handling of our pliable modelling material is most essential both in the early stages and throughout all levels of modelling. The first lesson has begun by harking back to our early school days, rolling and pressing the pliable material into various shapes, making anything that takes your fancy from sausage shapes to flights of your imagination. Practice all the time until you feel confident that the material is really under your control and you are ready to begin in the exciting task of modelling.

Model Kits

There are many model soldier kits on the market today both in metal and plastic form. These come with assembly and painting instructions and all these kits when assembled make very fine models. Some are shown in this book. The picture on page 23 shows the most important tools required to give the best results for the good finish which these excellent models deserve.

We will deal with the metal kit first. The most important job is to check the kit to see that all the pieces are there. The next step is to clean off all the seam lines on the metal pieces with a sharp blade, then smoothing the cut seam lines down with a small file. Having completed that job, the pieces should be tried out to see if they fit together, widening the neck and arm holes where necessary to ensure a good fit. Use an epoxy resin adhesive to glue the kit together. Not only is this an excellent adhesive, but it acts as a filler as well, thus by careful smoothing it obliterates any unseemly join lines. The glued pieces must be held firmly together. Any excess glue can be cut or filed off after it is dry. Fix the model to the base supplied, give the assembled figure a coat of metal primer and your model is ready for painting.

We now come to the plastic kit and this will take a little more time because of the many pieces involved. As each kit comes complete with well-drawn exploded diagrams, it is rather difficult to go astray.

The first task with a plastic kit is to see that everything is freed from the moulded tabs, then clean the flash lines and tab joining pieces. Join all the half pieces together, body, head, etc. As the plastic cement dries in minutes, no time is lost in being able to offer up the arms, legs and head to see if they fit. Having ascertained that everything fits perfectly, the leg pieces should now be attached to the body and then the feet firmly glued to the base. Apart from the actual sticking of the parts, the model from now on should be handled by holding the base only, especially during the painting operation. The head part is now assembled and placed on the body. In most plastic kits there is a choice of arm positions, either the at-ease or the shoulder-arms. The choice is yours. At this stage in the operation of assembling the model, you can either continue to assemble the equipment, or to paint the basic uniform. If you decide to do the painting, a light wash over the model with a detergent will help to prepare the surface for painting, and by the use of correct paints for plastic, a good result can be obtained. The final operation is the fitting of the equipment, which may be painted either before sticking on to the body, or after it is joined to the model. The latter is more difficult as the paint may overspill on the already painted surface of the uniform. Either way your model is now complete. As you can see from pages 46 and 47, a latex composition model can also be modelled in parts and the tools needed are not so different from those already shown. The only extras required are a tube of rubber-based adhesive and some fine sandpaper sheets.

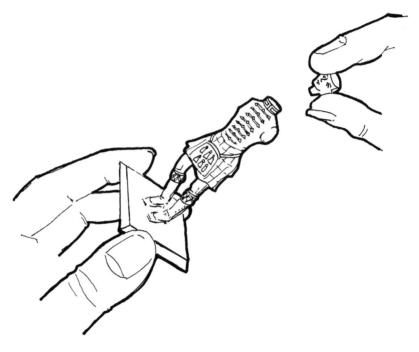

MODEL KITS (Fig. 1)
With the body now attached to the base, all future work on the model should be done by holding the base only, as illustrated.

A 30 cm Lancer in parts with an unmade sword and lance. The model is fitted with riding legs. On the extreme right is a finished sword blade without a hilt. This model, in kit form, is made from latex composition. The sword, hilt and lance are made from metal parts.

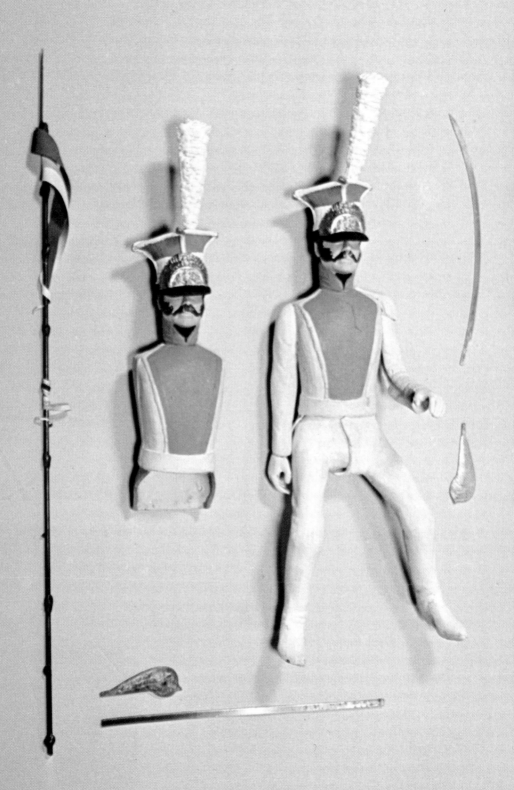

CHASSEUR A CHEVAL OF THE GUARD (Fig. 2)

A   Full dress shako of the 2nd Regiment of 1815. The head dress was scarlet and the pom pom and trimmings were yellow. In the centre was the tri-colour cockade fastened with a yellow loop. The peak and the couvre-nuque was black.

B.   This was the head dress of the Young Guard and was scarlet in colour. The shako plate was a large golden eagle. On the right hand side were orange coloured flounders and tassels. Across the front of the shako was an orange pleated cord ending in tassels which hung down on either side. In the centre was the tri-colour cockade over which stood a red over green plume. The peak was black and chin chain overlapping brass scales.

C.   The bicorne (1803–4) was in black felt and was used for walking-out dress. The hat was bound round the edges in black silk and the ornamentation was in orange colour. The tri-colour cockade was fitted to the right side with a loop of orange cord, from this issued a green plume surmounted with a red tip.

D.   Chasseur's Bonnet de Police 1813. This was worn for general undress duties, stables, etc. The overall colour was green with an orange band around the top of the hat which was edged in red. The long stocking shape hung from the right side and ended with an orange tassel. A central device was a bugle in orange.

E.   This was an Officers undress hat of the 2nd Regiment. It was rectangular in shape without a peak or ornamentation.

F.   The back view of the Chasseur's dolman.

G.   A Chasseur in the full dress uniform of service escort duty 1805–14.

H.   Pouch Belt.   I.   Carbine cartouche.   J.   Barrel belt front view.

K.   Barrel belt back view.   L.   Bugle-horn badge.

M.   Animation of a straight arm by cutting a notch in the elbow joint.

N.   The straight arm is now bent and formed into an animation or pose.

O.   The back of the pelisse as seen when hanging from the left shoulder.

P.   This was the undress coat of a trooper of the Chasseurs à Cheval. It was cutaway at the centre chest which revealed the scarlet waistcoat and hung down in tails at the back. The standing collar was red as were the cuffs and all the piping. The coat was green overall, the tails being piped red and at the extreme end of the tails was an orange bugle-horn device. Orange coloured cords and aiguillettes hung from the shoulder strap.

Q.   Austrian knot design for the trooper's breeches.   R.   Shoulder strap.

S.   Cockade with an eagle device in the centre.   T.   Shoulder strap.

U.   Flounders and tassel worn on the colpack.

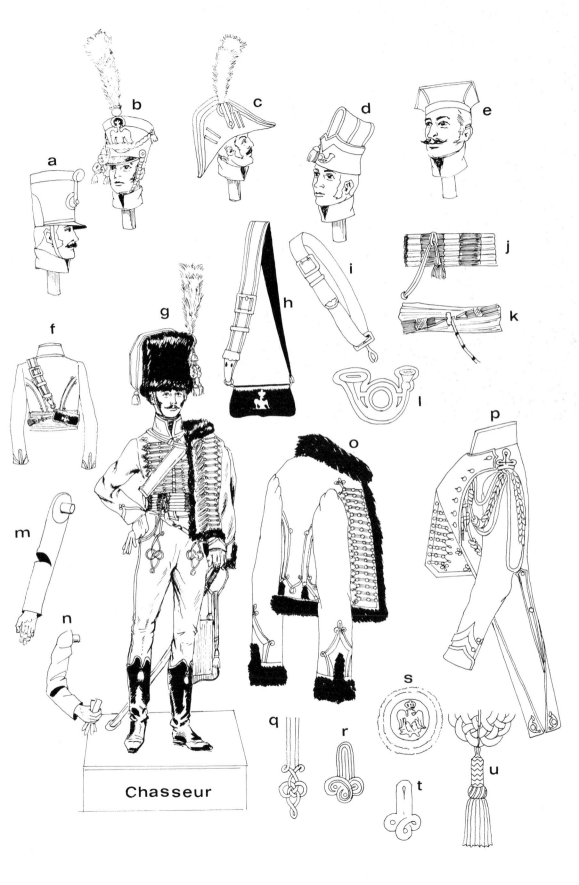

a

b

c

d

e

f

g

h

i

j

k

l

m

n

o

p

q

r

s

t

u

Chasseur

Left
A fine detailed metal kit of a British Infantry soldier of 1814, made by ALMARK, London, England.

Below
Four models in the 30 cm range made from latex composition. From left to right:— a British soldier of 1914, a British Officer of 23rd of Foot 1790, a Paratrooper of 1944 and an Artillery Officer of 1917.

An AIRFIX British mounted Hussar in plastic kit form is shown with an electric soldering iron, fitted with a plastic welding head and a cutting knife for trimming the 'flash' lines.

Layout of tools required for plastic and lead model assembly and conversion. Left to right:— a small metal cutting saw, skiving knife for trimming, a cutting knife, tubes of epoxy resin, files, a watchmaker's screwdriver, small screwdrivers, electric soldering irons, a coil of core solder, some metal model figures and, on the extreme right, a ROSE MINIATURE mini-pak.

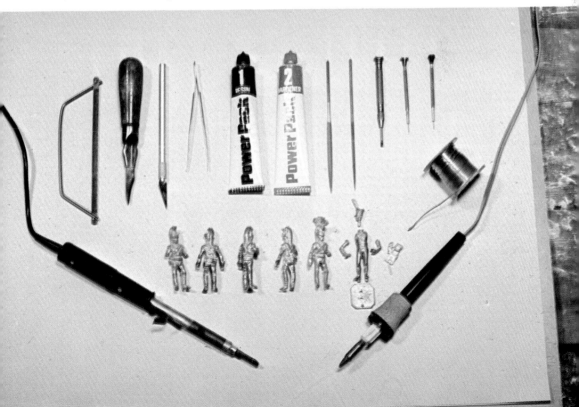

Converting

Like every other aspect of model soldier collecting and modelling, converting is no less a science of patience, practice and skill. The study of conversion is not without its pitfalls. To create a model of one's own choosing from limited parts, demands much from the creative ability of the model soldier enthusiast. To change a standing figure to a running position seems to be a simple problem, but where to cut, how deep to cut and finally how to cut? These are the important questions so study well before making even the smallest nick in your precious lead or plastic model soldier. The cost of converting could be the 'lives' of two or more models which have to be cut up and stripped of various pieces of equipment, even to their heads and arms, for 'replanting'. Think before dismantling the figures if the alterations you are contemplating improves the movement or if it makes it look grotesque. It is too late once the knife has sliced through the model. To bend a straight arm on a lead model a 'V' shaped notch is cut on the inside of the elbow part of the arm, then it is slowly bent into the correct position, remembering that the deeper the cut the greater the resulting animated action. A plastic arm is very much easier, simply heat the cutting knife, cut a 'V' notch and fill in by smoothing the knife over the join. Equipment can be made from a variety of materials from balsa wood, for packs and pouches, to flattened pins for bayonets. Tassels and cords are easily made from fine wire fashioned over knitting needles. Crossbelts, etc. are made from thin sheets of metal.

Model horses come into the conversion range by the cannibalisation of two or more, cutting them in halves or even quarters if necessary. 'V' shapes can be cut just under the horse's head which can then be twisted to one side or downwards, whichever position is desired to suit your purpose. Reins can be cut from thin metal sheets. Thin plastic strips can be cut to scale to make the reining for the plastic type horses. Fine wire makes splendid manes and tails giving a feeling of movement when properly arranged. The feeling of a forward movement and action can be achieved by the careful bending of tassels and flounders, coat-tails and sabretaches in a backward direction.

Most plastic kits consist of a variation of arms and equipment allowing for a choice without animating. Some metal kits are in pieces and the freedom of arm movements are also available.

The tools required are very little different from those which are used for making up a master detailed figure. The additions such as equipment, etc. can equally be applied to that of conversion and made from the same materials being glued and fastened in the same way. I have the normal

CONVERTING A HORSE (Fig. 3)
The position of the horse's head is changed by a V-cut in the throat and then slowly turning or bending the head into the required position. After positioning the head, the resulting gap is filled with an epoxy filler.

collection of craft knives, files, tweezers and a metal block with a small hammer (for beating out pins to act as spearheads and bayonets, etc.), and also a small electric pen soldering iron. Because of its many attachments the pen is very useful for both plastic and metal models. The 20 watt heating unit, shown on page 23, is fitted with several screw-on detachable heads. In plastic modelling the simple action of placing the smallest head of the iron onto the inside of the arm makes the plastic pliant enough to be bent into any position, legs can be treated in a like manner. The folds and crease lines can be re-introduced by the application of the heated iron. Bearskins can be remodelled and hair can be made to appear dishevelled when in action.

Similar to the metal models when spare off-cuts can be placed back into the melting pot and used again on a future occasion, so also can the off-cuts and sprue from the plastic kits be made serviceable again. The purchase from your local pharmacy of some carbon tetrachloride (which is quite an unpleasant

25

chemical so please handle with the greatest of care) is poured into a glass jar with pieces of the plastic off-cuts and sprue added, allowing the two ingredients to mix. The lid of the jar is securely fastened down, a screw top is ideal for this purpose, then allowed to stand for a few hours. The solution turns into a liquid plastic which can be used to 'coat' materials such as old handkerchiefs and ribbons, etc. which when dry can be used as cloaks, crossbelts, reins, straps, etc. There are many splendid books on conversions and some of these you will find listed on page 148.

CONVERTING A HORSE (Fig. 4)

The mouth bits are made by boring a hole through the upper part of the horse s mouth and then inserting a fine wire which is twisted into shape with a pair of long-nosed pliers. The right hand horse has been cut to allow the position of the head to be altered.

A 30 cm high model of a Drummer in a latex composition. This model depicts a young drummer boy of the 77th Middlesex Regiment of the 1812 Peninsular War period. He is wearing the reverse colours of the regiment and the 'stovepipe' shako, which was worn by the British Infantry since 1800.

Modelling

The making of a figure in parts is not so difficult as it may seem at first. Firstly the head must be made. This is our unit of measure. So bearing this in mind the upper part of the body can be made then the lower part with the legs. Here the pose or attitude of the figure must be decided upon, as to whether the lower part should be in the riding, marching, reclining or standing position. The arms may be made straight and any animation can be made at a later stage. Here are a few simple hints before commencing the modelling which you may find of some help, using the head as a unit of measure:—

The average figure is about 6–7$\frac{1}{2}$ heads tall.

The head itself is roughly in three equal parts:—

(1) From the hairline to the eyebrows.

(2) From the eyebrows to the base of the nose.

(3) From the base of the nose to the chin.

Here are a few rough guide-lines for the body proportions:—

The arm including the hand is half the length of the body.

From just under the knee to the foot is the same distance as from the pelvis to just under the knee.

Equally the distance from the foot to the pelvis is the same distance as from the pelvis to the top of the head.

The arm from the wrist to the armpit is roughly three hands long.

A hand is the length from the base of the nose to the hairline.

These proportions must be considered as a very rough guide only to begin modelling, naturally they do not conform to everyone, that is what makes us so individual and different. Working with these proportions in mind draft out on a simple sketch the essential pose and balance with the required measurements.

For the larger 30 cm figures it is advisable to build an armature or frame to support the heavy plasticine. If however you are making the model in kit-form each piece will be fairly solid, so it is not strictly necessary to build an armature. It is a good exercise however to build a frame because if plasticine is not available modelling clay can be used. Apart from the armature the modelling techniques of both clay and plasticine are the same. If anything larger than 30 cm is contemplated then the building of an armature and the use of clay is essential.

A figure-iron should be screwed to the base board with the supporting horizontal arm firmly screwed in and held fast. It should be set at a height that will support a figure from just above the waist for a full figure, but just about centre back when modelling a half figure as shown on page 31. The short moveable extension arm is placed in the vertical position and screwed tightly in. As we are making for this exercise a kit-form model only, a very simple type of armature is all that is necessary as the picture on page 30 clearly illustrates. Take a length of 2·5 mm square aluminium wire of about 18 cm in length and with a pair of long nosed pliers bend over one end about 25 mm to form a shepherd's crook, then with a finer wire such as 15 amp fuse wire, bind the armature wire to the small vertical upright moveable extension. Cut a length of armature wire roughly 35 cm long, bending to form a 'U' shape, invert this shape and attach the centre of the curved part to the upright of the armature wire and to the vertical upright, the shape now represents the head, shoulders and body, including enough depth for the base. This armature is very necessary for clay but not wholly necessary for plasticine modelling in this size.

The first layer of plasticine must be applied to the model at the centre (page 30 lower picture) and the flow of work must be from the centre up and down at the same rate of progress. The head at first being merely an egg-shape, but within this egg-shape must be built up all the features in proportion to the rest of the figure. No modelling tools are required at this stage, only your fingers should be used to build up and pack the plasticine around the armature.

The head egg-shape must be placed at an angle on a cylindrical shape which will be the neck. On this simple egg-shape draw with a wire-ended tool a line down the centre, then divide it horizontally into three equal parts, these represent the brow, the length of the nose and the mouth and the chin. Mark in the position of the ear with a large headed pin. The distance from the tip of the nose to the brow being the size of the ear and the base of the ear being just above the 'hinge' of the jaw. Starting from the top horizontal line build out the forehead blending upwards into the basic egg-shape always keeping a roundness in your modelling. All the features are governed by the forehead, if this is wrong the face itself will be incorrect. Check that the forehead is at the correct angle and is the right width and height. Now within the next section build up the cheek bones. Like the forehead these are important parts as they are the fixed bones of the skull and the 'scaffolding' of the face. In the third section of the head blend the chin line on the marked horizontal line back towards the jaw line to the position of the ear marked with a pin. Now check the basic form from the top and from underneath and also check the roundness of your handiwork. This being to your satisfaction proceed with building on the mouth structure. From about two-

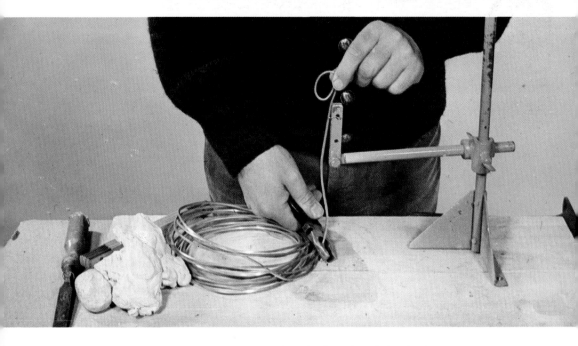

With the figure iron firmly secured to the base board the simple armature of aluminium wire is first shaped around the vertical arm and formed into a rough shape of the figure to be modelled.

The first plasticine in place on the armature, and working from the centre, building up in either direction.

Packing and forming the plasticine around the armature to reach the first stage in the making and building up of the model.

Smoothing in the detail and marking in the necessary equipment positions required for the final stage of a model of a Chasseur a Cheval.

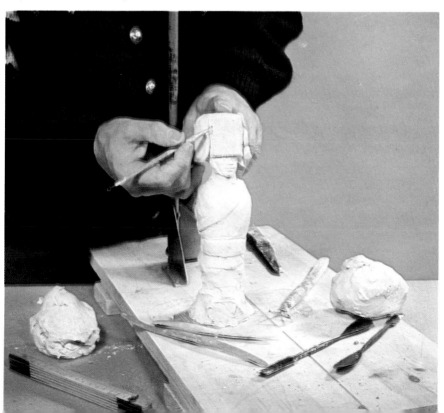

thirds up from the chin line start to build out the top lip, gradually blending to a point just over the second section where the base or the nostrils of the nose begin. This form should protrude further out than the cheek formation. The lower lip should now be formed, this projects a little further than the chin but not as far out as the upper lip. The cheek build-up forms the corners of the mouth. The nose may now be added; remember a nose has a front and sides. The bridge or the bony structure in the centre of the face is formed starting from just under the protruding brow build-up. The lower fleshy part of the nose projects a little further out than the bridge, this is supported on either side by two wing shapes which form the nostrils.

With small balls of plasticine the eyeballs are placed in position on either side of the nose. Over the eyeball shape place a thin leaf shape of plasticine which will form the upper eyelid which protrudes slightly over the top of the eyeball, but allowing the eyebrow build-up to project just that little further. Repeat the process at the bottom of the eyeball blending the bottom of the leaf piece into the cheek form. Remember that the upper eyelid is the heavier therefore projects just that little more. Last of the features to be added are the ears, these should have very special attention as apart from their great individuality with all those winding contours and folds they are rather difficult to model, so study very carefully a 'live' model from all angles to get these right. The head and neck column are now finished, the head without hair may look strange, but this is of course only a temporary stage. The hair or headgear of some sort can be now added and it is naturally governed by the period of the model you are making. A constant change of position whilst modelling the head helps you to see if you are correct in your modelling forms by the differing shadow casts. A slight over-exaggeration of the features in the early stages is not to be condemned, it is far better to have an exaggeration than a flat insignificant 'blob'.

Because of the small detail, a good hint on the smoothing down procedure is to dip a No. 2 paint brush into some paint thinners and gently 'wash' the face all over. One brushful is sufficient and if applied carefully, smoothing off any edges around the ears, nose and eyes, the face surface will be smooth allowing for easier and better painting after casting.

If the head is to be made as a completely separate piece of the kit the armature would need to be quite different. A length of dowel of 1·5 cm in diameter would be required. This should be about 15 cm long and at one end a number of tacks should be driven in covering an area of about 5 cm, this will act as the core armature. This is then covered with plasticine into the egg-shape build up of the head, following the instructions as previously described. The dowel acts as the armature and handling stick, by holding it in the hand and turning it at will, modelling becomes that much easier. Being on the stick the variation of light is achieved by a mere twist of the hand instead of moving from one position to another. After the model has been completed, place it in a vice and saw off about 7 cm of the dowel stick. Cover the sawn off part which retains the model head, with plasticine; this becomes the 'pour hole' for our liquid composition. Place the model on to a sheet of glass or a marble slab and smooth the plasticine from the model to the base, ensuring that it is firmly and securely held in preparation for the next stage of the procedure, that of making the mould. The modelling of the half body is not too difficult with or without the head being an integral part of it. This is a rather solid affair which in the first stage is made without any detail whatsoever, the important things are that the neck size, shoulder width (without arms), length of the body and waist measurements are correct also that there is a base on which the body stands, this being the pour hole for the composition. That is the easiest part of the body modelling. With a small wooden spatula mark on to the body the necessary ornamentation, such as buttons, frogging, etc., but before actually placing on the various items the actual uniform itself must be dealt with. The uniform has a texture which is most important and also it must be modelled so that it indicates that there is a form underneath. The creases and folds must express a living movement and action. It should look fresh and smart for parade, and worn, torn and ruffled if necessary, for some of the 'action' studies. After carefully modelling the folds and crease arrangements the various items of dress are applied as from the rough sketch and your compiled information on the uniform. These are now carefully modelled and painstakingly added, there are a few short cuts such as using large-headed pins for buttons, twisted fine wire for tassels and fringes, etc. which can be stuck to the plasticine. This is explained under the 54 mm modelling and conversion sections; as most of these ideas are universal in the making of model soldiers there is just a size difference.

The model is now set aside for casting.

Following our rough guide of proportions the legs are now modelled. The first and most important thing is the waist measurement, this must be neither too large nor too small and made in such a way that there is an extension of about 25 mm which when it is coated with adhesive will help both to bind and support the two halves when they are joined. The legs are now modelled with the folds and creases as indicated in your sketch, in the style of overalls, culettes, riding breeches with gaiters, hessians, etc. The soles of the feet are now the pour holes for the composition. The arms and hands can now be modelled, here there is a choice, either you are prepared

33

A 30 cm latex composition model of a Punjabi Musalman of the 30th Punjabis. This model shows the popular long khaki shirt, or kurta, worn over the plus-four loose trousers. The kurta had pockets and shoulder straps with the British type military badges and buttons. The bandolier and brown leather waist belt was worn. Khaki coloured puttees and boots were worn and the Lee Enfield rifle was carried.

A 20 cm model of a Zulu Warrior of the inDlu-yengwe, or Leopard's Den, Regiment of 1879. The model is made in a latex composition. The Zulu army was formed under the leadership of King Shaka when he came to the throne in 1816. By 1879 it had grown to a strength of 50,000 warriors. It was finally defeated at the battle of Ulundi on the 4th July 1879, by the British.

to make a number of arms in varying positions or to make simply a straight arm and to convert or animate them at a later stage. The animating and conversion is explained in another section but the principle is the same regardless of the ultimate material used for the finished model.

A length of armature wire is cut in proportion to the length of the arm of the figure being modelled and at one end are attached (either by adhesive or by twisting around) five pieces of fine wire which are spread fanwise out from the end, this is the armature for the fingers and hands. The arms in themselves are not too difficult, remembering that they too have folds and creases in the material, and in the right places. A straight arm naturally is the easiest by far, the pour hole should be situated at the shoulder joint. A small extension of about 15 mm is sufficient, this in the final assembly may be cut off, or a similar aperture cut into the shoulder arm hole and the extension piece glued and inserted, the join being filled in with an epoxy resin or some other like substance. The hands are not so easy, these are, next to the face, one of the most expressive parts of our body and it is said that they betray a person's character; thank goodness our models are too small for us to try to achieve that almost impossible task. From the sausage shapes, which must first be placed on the fine armature wire, they must be so constructed that they do not appear to be just sticks or lumps but rather as well formed pleasant and elegant shapes. Study your own hands and those of your family and friends and the knowledge you gain will be well worth while.

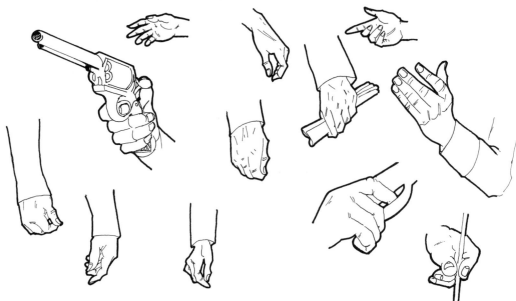

MODELLING AND ANIMATING (Fig. 5)
Illustrated are numerous hand positions which can, with careful manipulation, be achieved from the standard hand casting.

54 mm MODELLING

The making of the simple basic figure for the 54 mm size in plasticine is very uncomplicated if the forementioned proportions are followed. There is no armature whatsoever to be built and from several small plasticine shapes your figure can be made, making sure that your first egg-shape which is the head, is about 8 mm, and with this unit of measure, the rest of the body is made to conform. Although this is a basic form the general shape must be correct, if it is not, then the later process becomes an even greater problem. So working constantly with a pair of dividers checking and rechecking all the time get the proportions right. Obviously it is not possible to be able to model very fine detail with plasticine on such a small scale within an area of 8 mm for the features of the head or on a surface of approximately 6 mm for a well defined hand so the finer detail must be etched out when the basic model form is in another material, such as plaster, the next stage which is explained later.

Nonetheless the main features must be clearly defined, the main folds of the uniform material can be modelled in and a clear indication of where the trousers end and the gaiters or boots begin can be shown. With the blending of the forms and shapes together by working carefully and methodically as described you will see on examination how the form begins to grow, each shape joining the other at varying angles and by doing so creating the basic pattern of your model soldier. For the convenience of the later stages it is advisable to model your figure so that the arms are well away from the body and the legs running in parallel with the arms in the 'at ease' position, this allows for easier animation when the metal stage is reached. Having ascertained that all the proportions are correct and all the details of the main parts have been clearly marked in, including the extremities like hands and feet, then with a careful 'wash over' with a brushful of paint thinners to smooth all the hard edges which may have been left in, the model is ready for the first casting process.

Upper Left.
A painted and unpainted trooper of the German Africa Korps.

Upper Right.
German Officers in leather coats.

Lower Left.
German ski troopers of World War II, painted and unpainted.

Lower Right.
A superbly detailed and painted model of a German mortar and crew. These figures are 54 mm and made in metal by LASSET, GREENWOOD and BALL.

Opposite page.
A 30 cm figure of a native Commandant, Nawab Sir Hafiz Muhammad Abdullah Khan, K.C.I.E. of the 15th Lancers (Cureton's Multanis) of the Indian Army. The figure is made in a latex composition. It was quite common to call regiments after the names of their commanding Officers and although this practice had ceased in the British Army since 1751 it was carried on in the Indian Army.

FIGURE MODELLING (Fig. 6)

This plate shows the proportions of the figure.

A. The full figure is shown made from the shapes pictured at the bottom in Figure E. This shows the basic construction with the egg-shape on the cylinder which is attached to the thoracic block and the upper torso. The legs support the pelvis block and the arms join the upper torso block.

B. The muscle formation is marked in and the hard edges of the cubes are rounded off. The instructions for the head should be followed closely during the building of the body as outlined in the modelling section.

C. The head and body should now be in a half-finished state. Here, with the help of dividers, all proportions must be checked as beyond this stage it will be very difficult to correct any faults.

D. The finished figure. Check and smooth off all harsh edges.

E. Shapes to practice with.

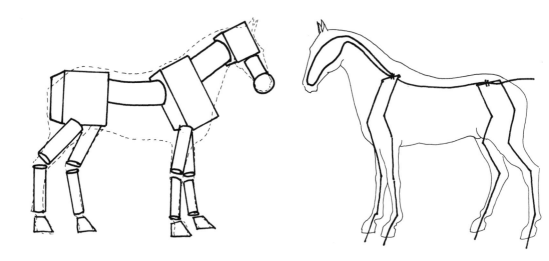

MODELLING (Fig. 7)
Illustrated here are the two types of modelling. On the left is a horse built from the cube and tube process and on the right a horse with a simple wire armature. Both methods can be used very successfully.

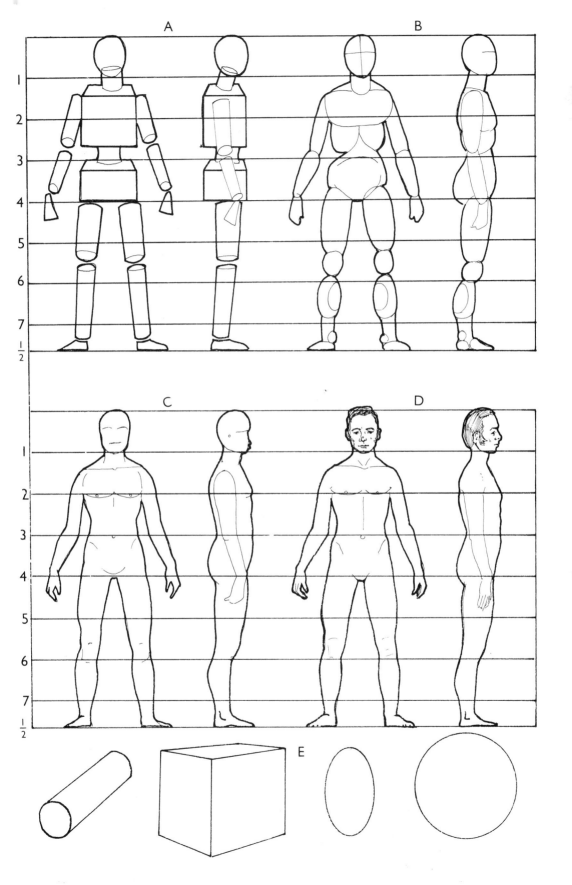

See page 44 for caption

The model illustrated on page 42 is 30 cm high and made of latex composition. It is of the British 'Tommy', a soldier of the City of London Regiment of the 1915 period. The khaki, flat topped field service cap was still being worn in action but was later replaced by the steel helmet. The gas mask was not yet a part of the soldiers' equipment.

On page 43 is a 30 cm model in latex composition of a British Artillery Officer of 1917. He is wearing the soft topped cap (the wire being removed) and the 'British Warms' which carried the badge of rank on the shoulder straps. Bedford cord breeches with boots and gaiters were worn.

Making and Casting

(Figs. 8, 9, 10 and 11)

A. The tools necessary for the modelling of 54 mm models are shown, consisting of wire-ended tools, spatulas of wood, and a pair of dividers.

B. Practise by rolling the plasticine in your hands and getting the feel of it by kneading and shaping it into simple forms.

C. The simple forms such as egg shapes, spheres, sausage shapes, cylindrical and in fact, any shapes.

D. By the use of a long knitting needle, making this the armature for your miniature figure and placing on this the various simple shapes, gradually build up a body, always keeping to the proportions as explained on pages 28 and 29. Do not be discouraged if your first figures are not as successful as you would wish them to be, simply roll your material back into a lump and start again. Remember, practice is all-important in the art of making model soldiers.

E. Remember to use your dividers constantly for the measurements and proportions of the body, taking a note of the rough guides.

F. A detail of the face and head, again taking careful note of the proportions.

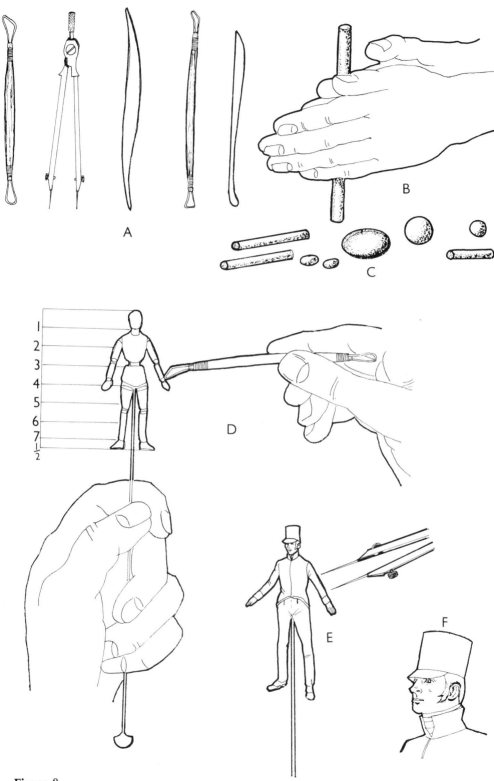

Figure 8

This is the plaster mould made for the latex composition pouring, and shows the body of a Chasseur a Cheval taken from the mould.

The legs of a Chasseur a Cheval made by the same method. Not shown are the hands, arms and the pelisse which are also made by the same process.

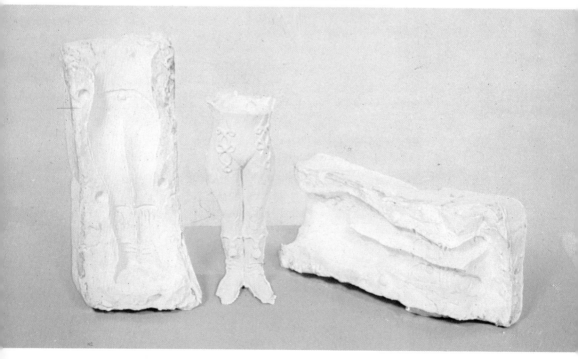

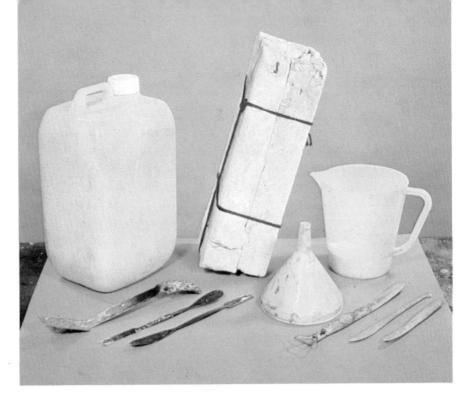

A plaster mould bound up and made ready to be poured into with the liquid latex composition, the plastic funnel and jug ensure there is no wastage of the composition.

The result of the pouring, a figure, minus legs, of Napoleon which can be seen as a finished model on page 75.

G. The figure is now securely fastened on to a base of metal, marble or glass. The smoothing down procedure by brushing over the model with a paint thinner medium is now done. A careful application of this will remove all harsh lines and allow for easier casting. Take great care over the face and hands so that the minute detail is not obliterated.

H. The simple retaining wall of a thin metal cylindrical shape is now placed around the figure.

I. The cylindrical shape is now secured with string and plasticine is pressed around the base of the shape to prevent the vinamold compound from seeping out from underneath.

J. The hot vinamold compound is now poured into the cylindrical shape carefully, allowing the liquid to be poured between the model and the retaining wall. Our diagram shows an opened-up view of the process.

K. The string is now removed and the metal cylindrical shape is released revealing the solid vinamold mould.

L. The mould shape is now marked exactly centre, front and back of the model, across the top and down either side. Strips of plasticine are flattened out and placed on the dividing line then bressed firmly down and built up until the plasticine has formed a wall as in the diagram. Bend a sheet of thin metal into a screen shape which will enclose one half of the mould shape.

M. The edges of the metal screen enclosure are brought to the plasticine wall surrounding the vinamold mould and fastened by rolled pieces of plasticine, so joining them together. The first half of our plaster casing is now ready to be made.

N. Allow enough water in your plaster making receptacle to fill the cavity of the casing and proceed with the making of the plaster as described on page 60.

O. Remember to pour in a continuous stream, filling the cavity up to the top.

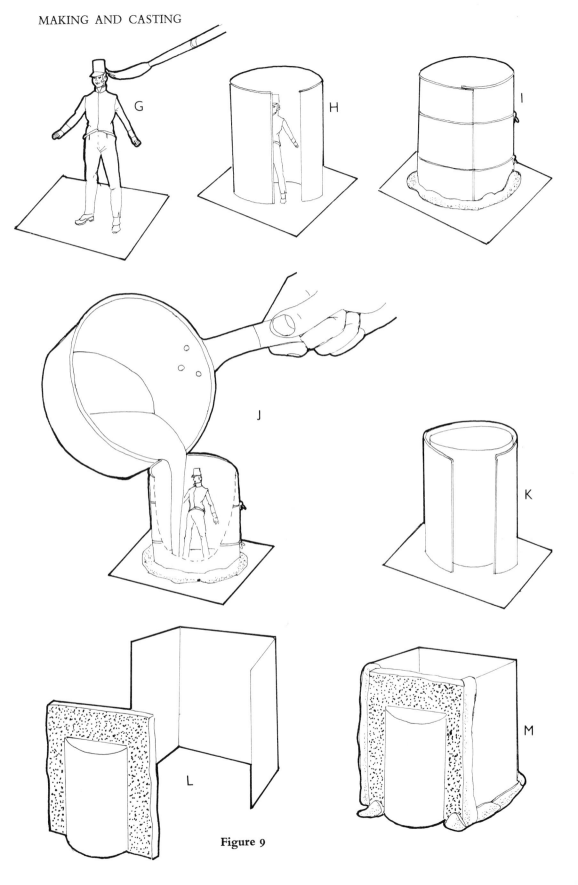

Figure 9

Above. This finely detailed plastic model of Napoleon mounted on his horse is made by the French firm of HISTOREX in the 54 mm range. Born Napoleone Buonaparte in 1769 in Corsica, he was the second son of a lawyer. First Consul of France in 1795 and crowned himself Emperor of the French in 1804. He abdicated and withdrew to Elba in 1814, and returned to Paris in 1815. He was defeated by the Allied Forces at Waterloo in 1815, he abdicated again and was exiled to St. Helena where he died in 1821.

Left. This model of Field Marshal the Duke of Wellington mounted on his favourite charger Copenhagen, is made in a latex composition and stands 45 cm high. Wellington was born Arthur Wellesley, the son of the Earl of Mornington, on 1st May 1769 in Dublin, Ireland. He defeated Napoleon at Waterloo on 18th June 1815. He was Prime Minister of Britain in 1827 and died 14th September 1851.

P. After about twenty minutes the metal screen should be removed and the plasticine wall stripped from the plaster face. The registration 'keys' are now scooped out of the plaster casing as shown in the diagram. The plaster wall still retaining the vinamold mould is given a covering of soapy water or household detergent.

Q. The thin metal screen is now placed around the uncovered half and, as previously, fastened with pieces of plasticine down the sides and around the base. To ensure complete support, string should be tied around the completed side of the casing and around the thin metal screen. The same procedure of pouring as in 'O' is now carried out.

R. The plasticine, screen and string are now removed and the mould is opened to ensure that both sides are a perfect fit. The mould is now re-assembled, tied with string and placed in the reverse position so that the feet are uppermost.

S. Having ensured that all parts fit perfectly the vinamold mould is removed and marked with a pen lengthwise around the mould, making sure that the line runs down the sides of the figure and not down the front and back. Now very carefully and with a very sharp blade cut the mould and extract the plasticine model.

T. The vinamold mould is returned to the plaster retaining casing and rebound with string.

U. With the mould and casing securely fastened, a plaster of Paris mixture, enough to produce a figure, is made up; an egg-cup full should be sufficient.

V. Here is a selection of tools required for the 'engraving' on to your plaster figure impression which will emerge from the vinamold mould. These tools can be bought, or in many cases be home-made. For example a strong sail-makers needle, when placed in a dowel stick shank makes an ideal engraving tool. Small files and fine sandpaper are also very important.

W. Making a careful marking out on the face, especially the thin divisional line of the lips. The eyes come in for a great deal of attention as do the nostrils and ears.

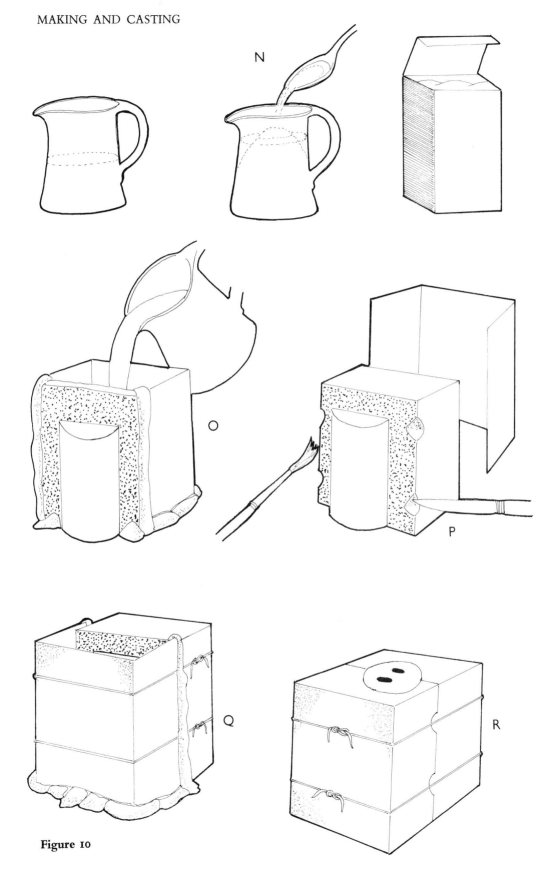

Figure 10

Above. This is a 15 cm superb model of a Risaldar or native Officer of an Indian Lancer Regiment of about 1900. This is a plaster model and was made in a world-limited issue of 70 models by HOWARD WILLETTS. It is mounted on a plaster plinth and fixed on to a wooden base, then enclosed in a perspex container.

Right. Models in 30 cm size show Indian Army figures made of a latex composition. They are of a Punjab Musalman of the 30th Punjabis and a Hindustani Musalman of the 1st Duke of York's Own (Skinner's Horse). The latter was formed originally in 1803 by James Skinner who was an adventurer who changed sides and joined the Indian Company, taking with him his old regiment. They were then called The Skinners Corps of Irregular Horse, then later the 3rd Skinners Horse, nicknamed the 'yellow boys'.

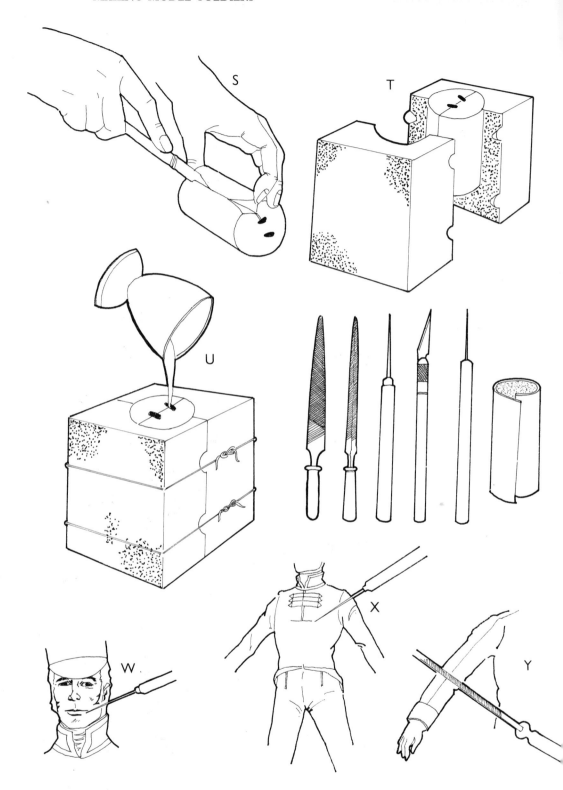

Figure 11

X. Here is shown the marking out of the lacing on the collar, coat and cuffs.

Y. File down any flash line which may have appeared, using the files and sandpaper very gently, as any undue harshness could ruin the figure.

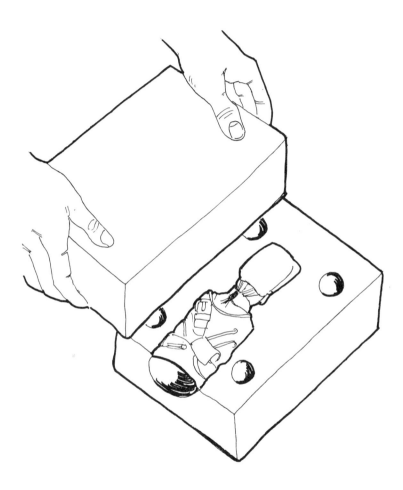

OPENING A MOULD (Fig. 12)
Illustrated is a mould of the 30 cm figures being opened.

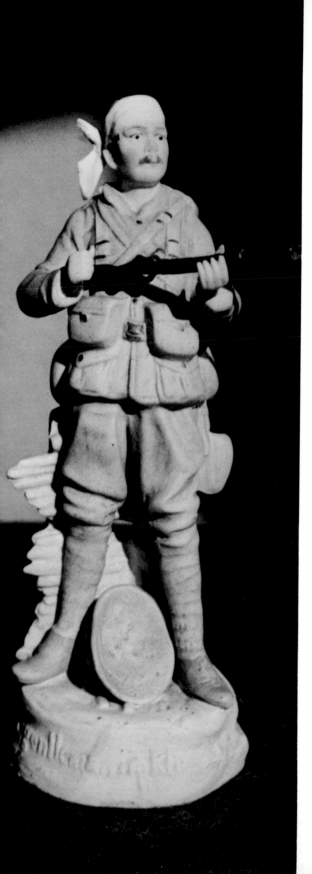

Right. A 45 cm high model of a mounted British 17th Lancer in his service undress uniform and wearing a foul weather oilskin cap. He is seen here in action during the famous charge at Balaclava during the Crimean War of 1854. The 17th was raised in 1759 by Colonel Hale who chose the Regimental device of the Royal Arms over the skull and crossbones and the motto 'or glory', thus their nickname the 'Death and Glory boys'. They became a Lancer Regiment in 1816. The model is made in a latex composition.

This fine 22 cm china figure is called 'Gentleman in Khaki' and was made in about 1902 from the painting by Woodville after Rudyard Kipling's poem of that name. This type of ornamentation was considered very patriotic to purchase during the South African War of 1899–1902. There were many examples of this kind of pottery and these are now collectors pieces.

VINAMOLD HOT MELT COMPOUND MOULDS

The finished model should now be securely fastened to a base which can be made from clay, metal or a marble strip. Retaining walls must now be erected, in its simplest form an oiled strip of paper or a sheet of thin metal formed into a cylindrical shape and secured with string can be used. The string is to ensure that the material does not unroll during the pouring of the hot compound. With the retaining wall or container now erected clay or plasticine should be pressed around the bottom of the cylindrical shape to prevent the compound from seeping and leaking underneath.

For the small quantities required, a saucepan of aluminium or stainless steel can be used as a melting pot. A source of heat readily available to the average model maker is of course the ordinary household electric or domestic gas cooker with an asbestos mat placed over the hot plate or naked gas flame. The vinamold should be cut into very small pieces and a handful placed into the saucepan on a moderate heat. It is now necessary and important to stir the compound frequently until all the pieces have melted and when this has happened then more pieces of vinamold can be added until the required quantity is reached.

With the vinamold in a completely liquid form, remove the saucepan from the source of heat and allow the liquid to cool to around 120 C, the manufacturer's instructions should be read and carefully carried out. The compound should be poured as quickly as possible and in one pouring without stopping, as an even stream. Bear in mind that at no time must the hot liquid be poured directly on to the model itself but between the model and the retaining wall, or, better still, against the side of the wall. As the mixture rises from the bottom upwards it forces the air from the finer detail of the model.

Before removing the model from the mould, a cooling time of some hours should be allowed for. To remove the model from the now flexible mould form it will be necessary to cut into the mould especially where there are deep under cuts. To contain this flexible mould form a two-piece plaster case must be made, this is explained under the rubber mould making section.

We are now ready to proceed to the next operation, that of reproducing our original plasticine basic model into a more permanent substance. A plaster of Paris reproduction will be admirable for our purpose to equip and make a detailed figure.

To meet our requirements we need the following materials and equipment:—

1 cup of plaster of Paris.

1 cup of water.   1 small mixing bowl.

1 wooden mixing spoon.   Vinamold plaster hardener (SP12).

The mould complete with outer plaster case is bound with string or strong elastic bands, and turned over with the feet openings uppermost, with the mould being made secure on the table.

Pour half the contents of the water into the mixing bowl, this should be sufficient for our needs. The amount of plaster hardener (if required) must be taken from the manufacturer's instructions. Now take the cup of plaster of Paris and with a to and fro movement over the mixing bowl sprinkle the plaster into the water. Continue to do this until the plaster is just below the surface of the water. Stir with the wooden mixing spoon until the mixture is of a nice creamy consistency and then pour the plaster steadily into the mould allowing it to run in against the side or wall of the mould.

After a waiting time of about half an hour the mould can be untied and the outer plaster case removed. Gently ease the flexible mould open and extract the reproduced basic figure of plaster.

Study the model very carefully for any air bubbles or blemishes.

Having ascertrained that no faults exist clean off any 'flash' which may, although this should be hardly likely, have attached itself to the model, with a fine file and very fine sand paper.

With all the relative information to hand of the type of model soldier required, including any rough drawings of uniform and dress equipment that may be used, the model may now be 'worked on'.

Most students shy away from what seems quite a difficult procedure although it is with practice a far quicker method for applying detail than any other I know. Here must be applied the techniques of an engraver with the aid of the metal and the simple wire-ended spatulas.

The metal tools should gently scratch away at the surface of the plaster, marking out the folds, creases, seam lines, openings and slashings, etc. of the tunics and breeches. The face can now receive more attention regarding the features making them sharper and more defined. The hands can also come in for the same treatment especially the fingers. Now to the fine detail of the uniform. Small pin heads make excellent buttons, these can be cut and glued into their respective positions. Sheets of tin or lead foil can be utilised for so many purposes, e.g. waist sashes, crossbelts, cartouches, cloaks, carry-straps, blanket rolls, shakos, cap peaks, saddle cloths, epaulettes, etc. From fine wire can be made in various ways plumes, feathers, fringes for the epaulettes, cords and tassels, etc. Small blocks of wood can be cut and made into packs. All these detail pieces can be fixed to the basic model with epoxy resin adhesive. I recommend that all weapons like swords, rifles and bayonets, unless the latter are made close in to the body, should be made in separate moulds as also should sabretaches because these would be rather difficult to extract from the rubber mould which is the next step in our model making.

A painted HISTOREX plastic kit assembly of a Royal North British Dragoon (Scots Grey) of 1815, and stands 54 mm high. Famous for their charge in the battle of Waterloo alongside the troops of the Highland Regiments who clung to their stirrups, they captured the French Colours. They were part of the Union Brigade under the command of Major General Sir William Ponsonby. The distinctive bearskin was decorated with the white horse of Hanover at the back.

A splendid 77 mm model in metal of a mounted Life Guard, Egypt 1882. The Life Guard is wearing the foreign service helmet with a puggaree. The Guards saw service in the Nile Expedition. They carried the Martini-Henry rifle Mk III and bayonet of 1879. The model is made by SERIES 77.

COLD CURING RUBBER MOULD MAKING

Because of its heat resistence and negligible shrinkage cold-curing silicone rubber is ideal for the model soldier enthusiast in preparing moulds for the making of metal and plastic type models. This room temperature curing silicone rubber can be purchased at most good art stores. The rubber compound is mixed with a catalyst (this is supplied along with the compound), which will accelerate or retard the curing time, according to the manufacturer's instructions which must be followed very carefully.

Having added all the detail to our model we now have to prepare it for the rubber mould. As plaster is a porous material it must be sealed although this is not strictly necessary when using the cold-curing rubbers. During cold weather however, it is advisable to slightly warm the now master model, as the air in the model, on becoming warm will expand and cause bubbles when contact with the compound is made. A thin coat of a good liquid detergent solution brushed over the completed model and allowed to dry thoroughly will be sufficient to act as a seal.

The preparation of the master figure for making a mould for low-melting metals casting is as follows:—

The simplest mould is the one-piece mould. Place the model on to a bed of plasticine, the bed being the depth of the vents or pouring channels attached to the model's feet. The plasticine base will anchor the model down and prevent it from rising and floating away when the liquid rubber silicone is poured in. Now build the retaining wall in much the same way as for the Vinamold mould, forming a sheet of thin metal into a cylindrical shape then securing with string or a piece of wire wound round and twisted at the ends with a pair of pliers. The bottom of the retaining wall can be attached to the base by using rolls of plasticine pressed firmly round, this not only secures the wall but the fluid rubber is prevented from flowing from underneath.

The cold-cure silicone rubber compound and catalyst comes with complete manufacturer's instructions which must be adhered to very carefully. It is easy to make and easy to use and will reproduce faithfully your master model down to the finest detail. Following the manufacturer's instructions the catalyst must be thoroughly mixed into the silicone rubber by hand stirring. During the mixing great care must be observed to avoid trapping excessive air. The normal time for the rubber to reach the handling stage is roughly ten minutes but this naturally depends on the amount of catalyst used and the room temperature. Remember that the rubber will start to cure as soon as the catalyst has been dispersed in the rubber compound. The humidity and temperature play a decisive part in the drying times, low temperature and humidity will slow down the curing time whilst high temperature and humidity will speed up the curing time. Depending on the room temperature, the normal curing time of the compound is twenty-four hours (I recommend a further twenty-four hours for the full properties to be attained). When the handling time of the silicone compound has been reached the job of pouring begins. The direction of the flow of the pouring must either be down the side of the retaining wall or between the model and the wall, never directly over the wall itself. The compound should preferably be poured all at once and in a steady stream. If however there are some deep undercuts on the model it will be necessary before pouring to brush some of the compound mixture onto these parts immediately before pouring; this will help to eliminate unwanted bubbles. The pouring should be continued until it has covered up to 13 mm over the top of the model. After making certain that the base holding the liquid mould is standing level, leave the mould to cure for forty-eight hours.

When the silicone rubber mould has cured, remove the cylindrical retaining wall of metal and your master model figure is now completely enclosed in a solid cylinder of rubber. Now prepare a bed of plasticine allowing plenty of space to accommodate the size of the mould plus at least 25 mm all round. Mark with a felt tip pen a line lengthwise around the mould, giving us the half way mark for the plaster mould. Make very certain that the line marked runs down the sides of the figure and not down the front and back, otherwise the seal line from the casting will spoil the features of the face and other details on both front and back of the model. Now embed the mould into the plasticine bed up to the ink mark after roughing up the smooth surface wall of rubber by making indentations into the mould so that the plaster will have sufficient 'keys' to retain the rubber mould in position. A retaining wall is now built around the plasticine bed and the embedded rubber mould. Registration 'keys' are scooped out of the plasticine bed one near each corner. Make up some plaster into a creamy consistency and spread it over the mould to a thickness of not less than 25 mm and if necessary make up a further bowl of plaster to fill the area of the box to the same height. As soon as the plaster is dry, reverse the mould and remove the plasticine bed. Brush the plaster surface with either soapy water or detergent and allow to dry. Build another retaining wall and repeat the process over again, then set aside to dry.

Remove the now dry plaster case from around the silicone rubber mould. Place the rubber mould on a bench and with a sharp knife cut open the mould along the centre parting line which is marked in ink. The ink mark

A plastic HISTOREX model of a French trumpeter of the Lauzan Legion who fought in America during the War of Independence of 1776. The model stands 54 mm high. There were many volunteer French troops fighting alongside the American colonists who were fighting for their independence from the British Crown.

Right. A SERIES 77 metal model of a French Hussar Trumpeter of the 5th Regiment of 1809. As the name implies the basic figure is 77 mm high, a little larger than the more popular collectors pieces of 54 mm, the larger size does in no way detract from the perfect detail. On the contrary, the result will satisfy any serious collector.

has now served two purposes, that of dividing the plaster and the other of showing the cut-line for the extraction of the master model and the subsequent castings.

Before removing the master figure cut a conical shape out of the mould up to the base of the feet. This shape must not be wider than the outside edges of the feet as this now constitutes the pour-hole. Open the rubber mould which has just been cut and very carefully remove the master figure model, which should be equally carefully placed in a very safe place for any future use. Now replace the rubber mould back into one of the halves of the plaster casing, and scrape out a conical shape continuing from the rubber mould. When the process has been repeated on the other half, you should now have a continuous pour-hole through the plaster outer casing and through the rubber mould to the impression of the model. Before assembling the mould for casting a light dusting of graphite powder will help to give high quality castings. After dusting, place the rubber mould back into its plaster casing, secure with strong elastic bands. The mould is now ready to receive the first metal pouring. The method of low-melting metal casting is described under the section dealing with plaster mould making.

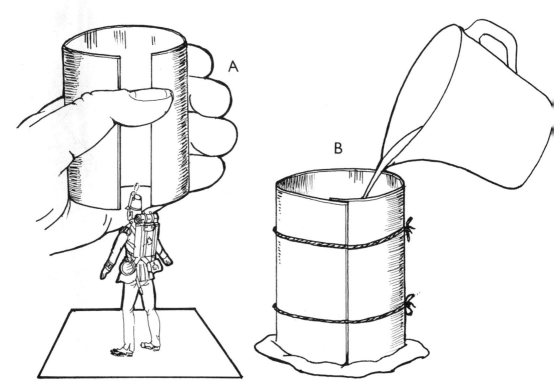

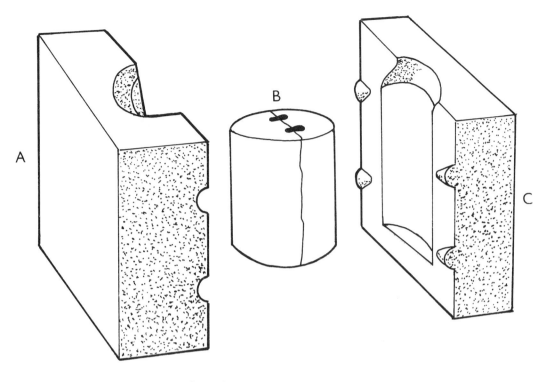

RUBBER MOULD (Fig. 14)

Illustrated is a rubber mould for lead or liquid plastic pouring.

A. The female half of the outer plaster retaining casing.
B. The rubber mould with the pour holes (through the feet) being uper-most.
C. The male half of the outer plaster retaining casing.

MAKING THE RUBBER MOULD (Fig. 13) *See page 68*

A. The equipped model is now fastened firmly to the base. A metal cylindrical shape is placed around the figure and securely tied with wire or cord.
B. The bottom of the container is sealed with plasticine and pressed hard against the wall to prevent any seepage. The liquid rubber is now poured in.

A 54 mm plastic model of a trooper of the Prussian Hussar, 'Death Head', 1st Regiment, 1808–14 made by HISTOREX of France. He is wearing the foul weather oilskin over the shako. After their defeat by Napoleon a full scale reorganisation of the Prussian army took place. The 1st and 2nd Leib Hussar Regiments were formed from Prittwitz Hussars in December 1808. Both wore black uniforms, the difference being white shoulder tabs for the 1st and red shoulder tabs for the 2nd.

A 54 mm metal figure of a French mounted Grenadier made by HINTON-HUNT. The Horse Grenadiers of the Guard were formed from the Horse Grenadiers of the Consulate. The uniforms were very little different from the newly formed Grenadiers of the Guard who were formed in 1804 and disbanded in 1815.

PLASTER MOULD MAKING

As the model is in a pliable material, e.g. plasticine, the procedure is as follows.

The model is mapped out into two sections using strips of plasticine or metal to form the fence or boundary. Once this is completed, enough plaster of Paris is mixed to commence work on the mould. Due to the smallness of the model the plaster is spooned on. When sufficient thickness of plaster has been laid on and the plaster is still soft, scoop out with your metal spatula a half-moon shape from both sides, two scoops from either side would be better; these one above the other to act as keys to ensure correct alignment when pouring. The half completed mould is left to dry out. When dry, the boundary strips are removed, any slight damage to the model made good and the surface of the half mould lightly washed over with soapy water or any household washing up liquid. The procedure is repeated for the other half of the mould. The mould is then set aside and allowed to dry. When dry, the mould is gently eased apart and the pliable model material removed. The mould is now thoroughly cleaned and all traces of the soft pliable material in the tiny crevices are very carefully removed with a wire-ended tool in order not to damage the detail which is so necessary on such a small mould. The mould is left to dry for some twenty-four hours. When completely dry, it is essential that there is no mixture whatsoever left in the plaster mould when the molten metal is poured in. This could be the cause of a 'blow back' which could result in an injury. You have been warned! Always ensure that the plaster mould is absolutely dry before commencing to pour the hot metal.

As all methods and techniques have their advantages and disadvantages, it is only then necessary to choose the simplest for your purpose. The following is another way to make a plaster mould. Apply three coats of 'Shellac' to the plasticine figure, allowing each coat to dry before brushing on the next. When the figure is thoroughly dry, this will form a hard outer covering to prevent damage when pressing it gently but firmly into the clay 'bed'. The figure should be marked with coloured ink or a felt tipped pen with a dividing line which is the predetermined half-way parting line for our two piece mould. This should be very carefully done to facilitate an easy parting. A 'bed' of 25 mm thick clay should be prepared, and the figure pressed firmly in up to the dividing ink mark. The clay is smoothed down tight up to the half submerged figure, allowing for the feet to be the pour holes. A depression must be made in the clay about 2·5 cm above the head of the figure by using the paddle end of the metal modelling spatula.

A conical depression can quite easily be scooped from the clay neatly and cleanly. This should be repeated on either side of the figure again about 2·5 cm away. These are the keys for the mould alignment.

It is now only necessary to brush lightly the half protruding figure with a coat of oil to prevent its adhering to the plaster. The bed of clay may be left untouched as it has its own resistance to the plaster. Surround the clay with a wall of either wood or plasticine. If wood is used, then a light coating of oil will also stop the plaster sticking. Mix the plaster of Paris as before to a fine creamy substance then, with the aid of a cup, pour the liquid plaster around the edges of the wall allowing the plaster to flow towards the figure. This must be a firm steady flow with no splashing, and on no account must you pour directly onto the figure. When the covering of the figure is completed, the plaster should be brought up to a thickness of about 2·5 cm. The half completed mould should be set aside and allowed to dry.

When it is dry, the mould should be turned over and the bed of clay, which is now uppermost, must be removed, revealing the back of the model figure embedded in the now plaster bed. Wash over the plaster with soapy water or detergent and lightly coat the back of the protruding figure with oil. The mixing of the plaster and the pouring procedure is repeated and the mould allowed to dry off. When completely dry the mould is eased apart very gently and carefully. With the separation of the two halves and the figure removed, the mould is ready for pouring. For casting, the purchase of a good quality metal ladle is the only piece of equipment necessary for the amateur model soldier maker. The choice of metal or the combination of alloys is really a matter of experience, but a low melting alloy is easier to handle and better for animation. The mould should be securely bound and placed safely on a bench or table in preparation for the pouring operation. Sufficient low melting alloy is placed in the ladle which is then taken to the heat source. Either gas or electricity can be used whichever is the more readily available. The correct time to commence the pouring is when the silvery surface of the metal begins to turn blue or brownish in colour. The best method is by pouring gradually and carefully, allowing only a few drops at a time to enter the mould. After the mould has been filled a few minutes should elapse allowing the metal to solidify. No time should be wasted in removing the casting from the mould as extended heat within the mould can be damaging to the impression. By gentle rocking and easing, the two halves of the mould will come apart leaving the metal casting in one of the halves. By the use of a pair of long-nosed pliers and applying the same gentle easing motion, the metal cast figure can be extracted.

73

A 54 mm HISTOREX plastic model of a Polish Lancer of the Guard. When Napoleon entered Warsaw in December 1806, he was escorted by a Guard of Honour. He was so impressed that in 1807 he formed four squadrons of Polish Cavalry.

Right. The Emperor Napoleon at Field Headquarters with his Officers holding a strategic discussion. In the foreground is a drum being used as a table and covered with maps. These are 30 cm high figures in a latex composition. Page 47 shows the figure of Napoleon in the making, used in this plate.

This reasonably cheap method of making a mould is not without certain drawbacks. Firstly there is the vulnerability of the mould itself. Being plaster and not very thick, it can easily be broken if not handled with great care. Secondly, the excessive heat of the molten metal destroys detail very quickly, lifting the surface off the plaster. I recommend the use of this method only if, (a) the amount of castings are few in number and no great detail is required, and (b) a basic figure only is required which will be cleaned up, greater detail added, and recast in a rubber mould.

BRITISH INFANTRY SOLDIER IN EITHER LEAD OR PLASTER (Fig. 15)

A. Engraved figure in lead or plaster, ready for the buttons.

B. Cross belts with cross belt plate.

C. Back view with the cross belts attached.

D. Shako with false front and hat plate and plume.

E. Water bottle and strap.

F. Epaulette and button.

G. Front view of finished model with equipment.

H. Shako cords.

I. Rear view of finished model complete with equipment.

J. Cross-belt buckled ends, cartridge pouch and regimental device.

K. Epaulette and button.

L. 'Brown Bess' rifle.

M. Bayonet scabbard.

N. Bread bag or side pack.

O. Shoulder straps with chest strap.

P. Bayonet (a beaten-out pin). Left is the pin unbent, the pin head is bent over and attached to the small funnel of metal.

Q. Back pack equipment

R. Backview showing shoulder strap arrangement.

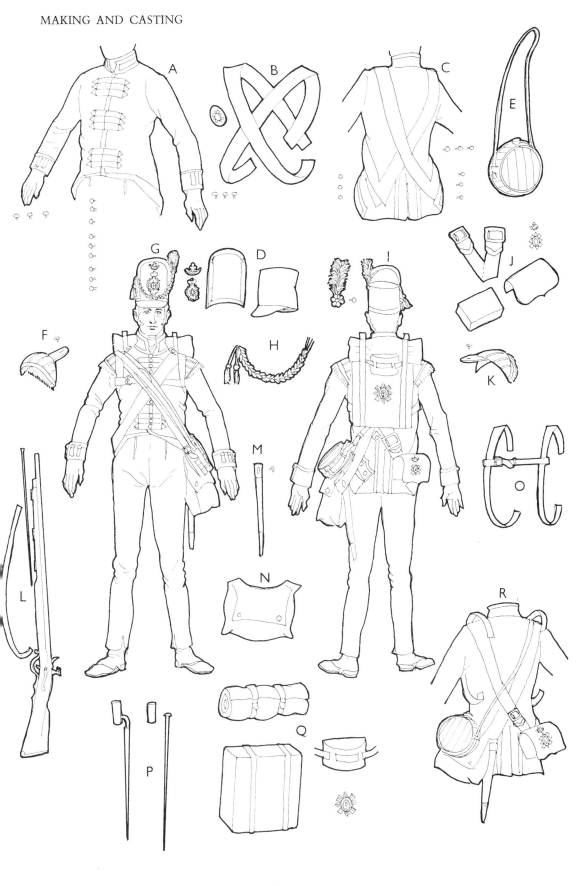

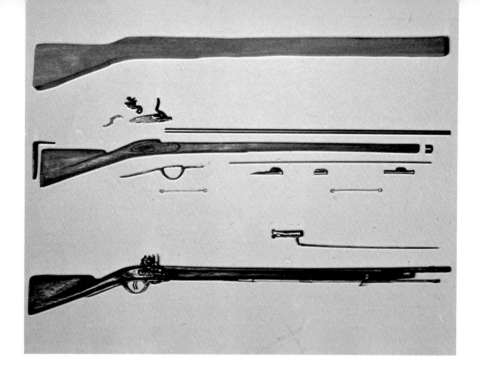

A model kit of the British 'Brown Bess', the standard musket with steel rammers which dated from 1730–80, is shown here with a wooden stock and metal parts, which consist of the lock, side plate, trigger guard, butt plate, sling swivels, rammer and muzzle, etc.

Below. A selection of toy miniature guns made by MARX of Swansea, Wales. It can be clearly seen that some of these models represent cavalry carbines.

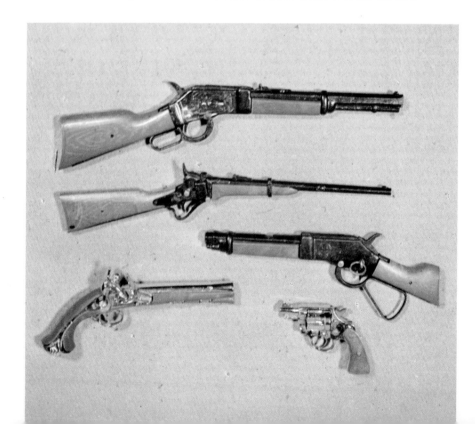

A

B

C

D

E

F

G

See page 80 for caption

PLASTER MOULD FOR METAL POURING (Fig. 16)

A. Place the 54 mm figure on a thin sheet of metal or glass. Mark out with a faint line around the figure up the right side, under and then over the arm, over the shoulder, up the neck, around the ear and up over the hat and repeat the whole procedure down the left side. Roll out strips of plasticine or clay and place them against the marked line and follow around. The marks for the registration 'keys' are made by cutting in with a wooden spatula.

B. Having surrounded the model in the medium chosen, mix sufficient plaster as previously described and spoon on, not allowing the plaster to fall directly on to the figure.

C. Remove the pliable medium of the dividing wall, coat the plaster face with soapy water and repeat the procedure of spooning on the liquid plaster on to the other half of the mould.

D. A side view of the model embedded in one half of the plaster mould.

E. The mould is cleaned of any particles which may have been retained whilst removing the model. It is now left to dry out thoroughly. It is very dangerous to pour hot metal into a plaster mould when it is in a 'wet' condition, a blow-back can cause injury. I therefore recommend this method mainly to those readers who have had some experience in the handling of lead and metal alloys.

F. When absolutely dry the two halves are brought together and then securely bound. The mould should then be firmly held by being embedded in plasticine. Then the pouring of the metal should be carried out with the utmost care and attention.

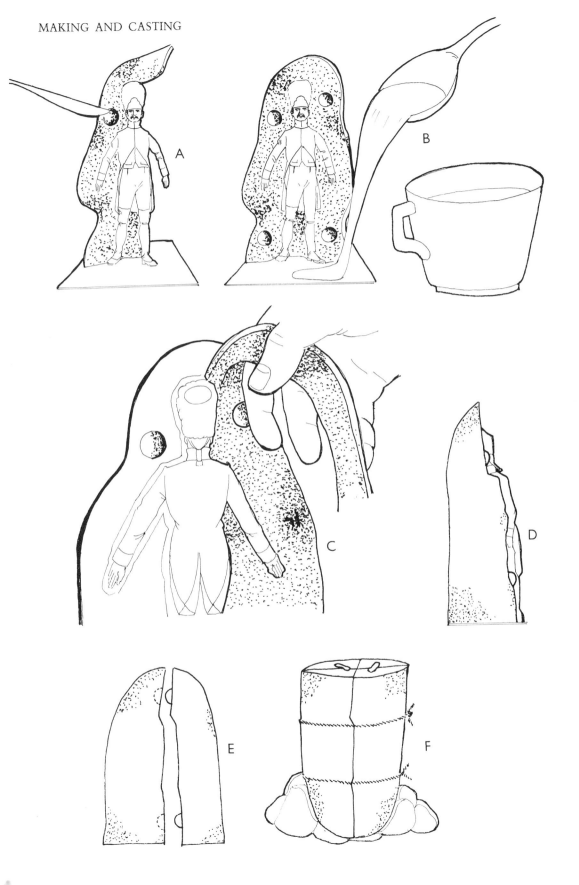

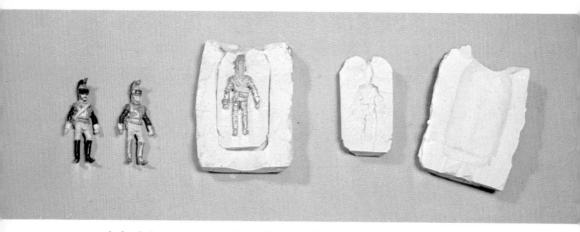

A simple home-made two piece silicone rubber mould with its plaster case and some of the resulting metal figures.

Below. Metal figure kits, one of a British Light Dragoon by ROSE MINIATURES and an American paratrooper by MERITE MONOGRAM MODELS Inc., Illinois, U.S.A. These are both finely detailed models.

Right. A 45 cm high figure in a latex composition of an N.C.O. in the 7th Regiment of von Malackowsky's Prussian Hussars of 1762. This was the typical Prussian/Hungarian Hussar uniform of the period with the black 'flugelmutze', replacing for a short time the brown colpack. The uniform remained, apart from minor alterations, the same as did the shabraque and sabretache.

PLASTER AND LEAD MODEL (Fig. 17)

A. The finished engraved lead or plaster model.

B. The plume is made from fine, thin wire, as also are the epaulettes and tassels.

C. The front and back views of the head and hat complete with the hat cords, flounders, tassels and plume, all made from the fine wire. Notice the grenade on the top of the hat.

D. The front and rear views of the coat. The buttons are pin heads which are cut and glued into position. Epaulettes and fringes are made from fine wire. The cross belts are made from thin metal strips or strips of thin plastic sheeting.

E. This is a detail of the back of the coat showing the pocket and turnbacks. The buttons are again pin-heads glued into their appropriate positions. The grenade emblems are shaped and also glued down.

F. The back pack is made from a small block of balsa wood and scribed with a knife to give it the 'fur' look. A roll of thin metal or plastic cut to size is ideal for the rolled blanket. The straps are either metal or plastic strips.

G. The cartridge box is made from a small block shape of balsa wood with a front cover of metal or plastic. The cover, which has the Imperial Eagle and grenades adhered to it, is cut a little larger than the wood in order to give an all over 'overlap'. The forage cap or 'Bonnet de Police' is a piece of rolled metal or plastic and fitted with a fine wire tassel, then glued to the underside of the balsa wood. The front cover is then placed over the wood and glued down.

H   The hat plate is a piece of metal cut to shape, engraved with one of the sharp needle tools and glued into position in the centre front of the hat.

I. If the figure is cast in lead or a metal alloy then animation of the arms can be achieved by nicking a groove in the elbow joint of the arm, the degree of the groove depending on the movement or animation required, the deeper the cut the greater the movement.

J. Another animation of the arm, this time a complete severance and the arm placed into the required position and glued with an epoxy resin or soldered.

K. The rifle. This must be a separate casting but the procedure is the same as for all rubber casting. First a plasticine model is made, then the subsequent rubber and plaster casing. Study your information very carefully.

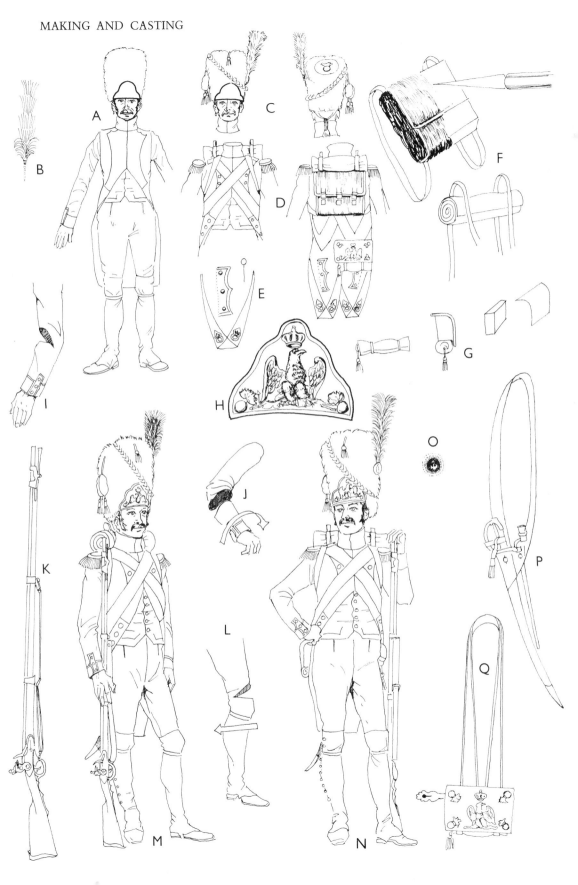

Left. Colourful uniformed 30 cm latex composition models of the Royal Regiment Drummers of 1751. By a warrant of 1751, the drummers were allowed to wear the Royal Livery. Until 1786 hanging sleeves were worn, hanging down the back. It is a little obscure as to the reason for these sham sleeves which were a fashion of the sixteenth century. The Grenadier cap which was worn had the galloping white horse of Hanover embroidered on the turned up front with the words 'NEC ASPERA TERRENT'.

This is a finely detailed and painted model of a British private of an Infantry regiment of the line of the 1815 Waterloo period, wearing the 'Belgic Shako and uniform as described on page 80. The model, in a metal alloy, is made by CHARLES STADDEN, the most prolific of the British model soldier makers.

A British Grenadier 'Red Coat' of 1776 during the American War of Independence, made in latex composition. The lack of understanding by the British Government of the problems of the British Settlements in North America caused a break-away by thirteen of the colonies and their declaration for an independence in 1776. By 1783 the United States of America was born.

L. Leg animation in metal is achieved in the same way as the arms, by cutting grooves into the appropriate position and remembering to cut into the opposite side to that you wish to bend.

M. A simple animated soldier, the arms being brought down to the sides and a simple cut to bring the left leg forward.

N. A greater animation with the one arm being placed on the right hip, the other supporting the rifle, the arm being bent at an extreme angle.

O. This is the tri-colour cockade which is fastened at the base of the plume.

P. The 'hanger' sword is a separate casting and should be carried out with the prescribed procedure. The bayonet is a beaten out pin and the top is a small cylindrical shape of rolled plastic or metal. This is then glued to the pin. The sword belt and 'hanger knot' are made from strips of metal or plastic.

Q. This is the Imperial Guard's cartridge box and rolled forage cap as described under 'G' in this section.

LATEX POURING (Fig. 18)
Here are seen the larger moulds for the 30 cm figures. This is a latex pouring with the mould being firmly and securely tied and the latex composition is being poured in with the aid of a plastic funnel.

LATEX POURING

The plaster master mould is now a true reproduction of the original model. Before pouring the latex, the plaster mould must be dried out thoroughly. The parts of the mould are now re-assembled ensuring that the registration keys fit exactly into each other. The mould is then securely tied together with string or bound with elastic bands. If it does not bind tight enough small pieces of wedge-shaped wood can be fitted between the string and the wall of the mould, thus pulling the string taut.

The composition comes from the manufacturer in liquid latex and filler paste form, and by varying the proportions of the filler paste to the liquid latex, the degree of hardness or flexibility of the finished model can be controlled. The two components are thoroughly mixed into a smooth paste and allowed to stand for about twenty-four hours to dispel air bubbles.

The mould is now slightly dampened before pouring in the composition. To minimise 'flash' a good tip is to pour a very small amount of the latex composition into the mould and allow it to run along the seam or joining line. This is then emptied out and returned to the container. To lessen the possibility of air bubbles the mould should be balanced at an angle of 45°. The mould is then completely filled with the composition at a steady flow, giving a gentle tap to the mould during this operation to assist the liquid in reaching the small and more detailed cavities. To allow for the drop in the level of the composition due to the absorption of the moisture from the compound by the porous plaster mould, a constant 'topping-up' must be carefully adhered to during this build-up period. Although the time for this build-up varies according to the shape and formation of the mould, a good time limit is about fifteen or twenty minutes.

After this lapse of time the mould should be inverted and the residue of the compound poured carefully back into the container for further use. The plaster mould containing the deposited rubber skin of the gelled latex composition on the plaster mould surface, can be either left in a warm atmosphere and allowed to dry out for a few hours, or be placed in an oven with a temperature of between 50° and 70° C which will dry it out (vulcanise) in about thirty minutes. Drying time again is governed by both the shape and size of the mould, and the filler loading. When dry, the mould is very carefully untied and eased gently apart and carefully dismantled.

After the casting has been removed from the mould it should be placed in a safe place and allowed to dry (mature) at normal room temperature.

When completely dry there is a shrinkage of about 10%. The 'flash' line, due to the liquid composition seeping into the seam lines of the mould, can be removed with sand-paper or a small inexpensive buffing motor.

A gunner of the Royal Horse Artillery with gun and limber. The gunner is 15 cm high and made of a latex composition. The gun and limber are made from wood and metal. Nicknames like the 'Galloper Guns' and 'The Flying Artillery' were gained by the R.H.A. because of their reputation for speed and efficiency whilst working in close co-operation with the cavalry.

Left upper. A German Anti-Aircraft gun of the 1939 period. This model is made from metal and is a replica of the famous German 88-mm Flak gun and used also as an anti-tank weapon

Left lower. British Naval gun of 1805 period made in wood and metal. This is a replica of one of the famous guns of the wooden fighting ships. Although by modern standards not very accurate they could nevertheless inflict a great deal of damage.

9-POUNDER FIELD PIECE (Fig. 19)

Here is a composite picture of the gun and the parts named.

A. Muzzle.
B. The chase.
C. Rivets.
D. Caps square.
E. Trunnions.

F. Vent.
G. Breech.
H. Button.
I. Elevating gear.
J. Nave.

K. Linchpin.
L. Tyre streak.
M. Felloe.
N. Trail.
O. Trail eye.

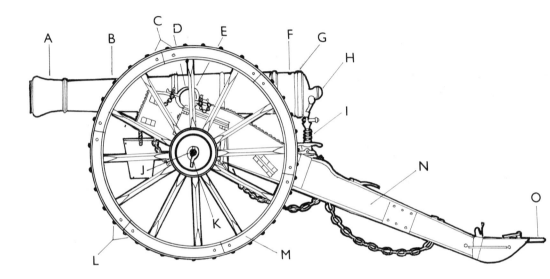

BRASS CANNON. 32 POUNDER (Fig. 20)

A. Brass barrel.
1. The muzzle.   2. The chase.   3. The trunnions.   4. The vent.
5. The breech.   6. The cascable.   7. The button.
B. Side view of the carriage.
C. Plan view of the carriage.
D. Quoin block and 'breeching' rope (which limited the recoil of the gun).
E. Tackles. Three of these were needed, one on either side of the carriage and one at the rear.
F. Sponge. This is a wooden handle with either bristles or a sheepskin head for cleaning the bore of the gun.
G. The rammer. Was used for ramming down the shot.

This model is made from wood and metal, although the barel can be cast in latex composition.

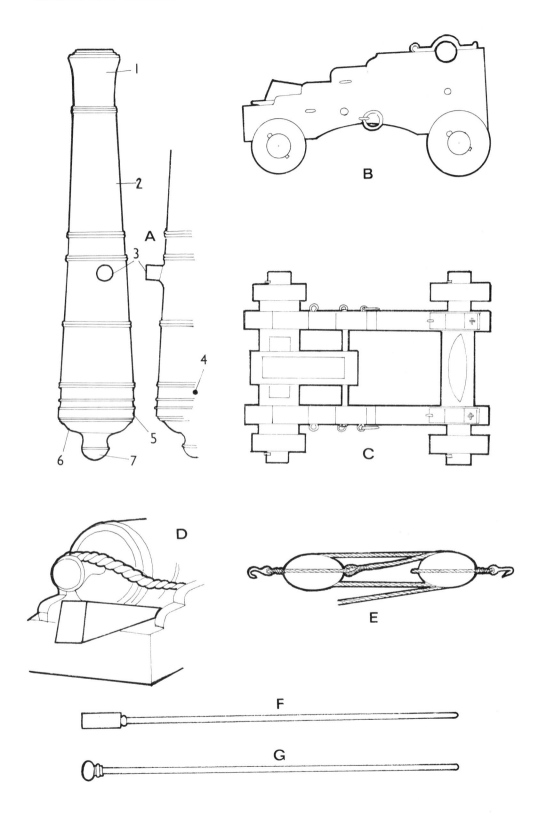

A 9-pounder field gun of the early nine-teenth century. The block trail was introduced by William Congreve and first saw service in 1792. It gave great mobility in turning and manoeuvring besides making it much easier to limber and unlimber, having this great advantage over its European counterpart. It was first used on 6 and 9-pounder guns but later became adopted for the heavier types of 12–24 pounders. It was fitted with bucket and wheel skid and chain. The brass barrel was replaced by iron after 1820.

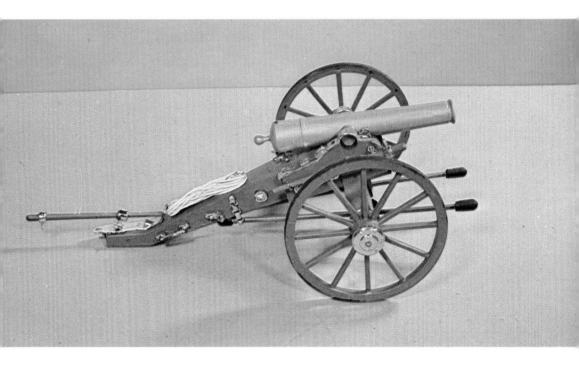

An American Civil War field gun produced in a plastic assembly kit. These 12-pounder bronze field guns were originally produced in France by La Place Freres in Paris, thus their nickname of 'Napoleons'. They weighed 1,200 pounds, and fired a projectile of $25\frac{1}{4}$ pounds, using a charge of $2\frac{1}{2}$ pounds of powder. They were eventually built at the Augusta Arsenal, U.S.A.

Painting

The technique of painting is like all other techniques, you choose the one which suits you best. My method, although being highly satisfactory for me and the one I describe, is by no means the only way of creating a satisfactory model in a finished painted state. Find your own technique, be it through short cuts or a time absorbing method, the final satisfactory completion of your model is the ultimate prize.

Our basic physical similarities are more or less the same but there it ends, we express our ideas and thoughts in different ways. Regardless of our differences we seek the elusive answer, perfection. This method is very simple and straightforward, paint so that the models take a character and a personality of their own. The method described is suitable for all types of models shown and explained in this book, regardless of the materials used. First the model is given a coat of white primer. It is advisable to make it thin enough so as not to obscure the detail and it is much better to give two very thin coats than a thick one. A good start is to clean your model of all grease marks which adhere to the surface, which come even just by handling. The best method here is to dip the brush into some of the paint thinners and 'wash' over the complete model, ensuring the removal of all traces of dirt. Allow this to dry, then apply the next coat of primer and set aside to dry again.

Brushes are very important, a cheap brush is useless and will give very poor results whilst a good brush will not only produce good results but will last just that much longer with the care that any good instrument deserves. For the smaller models and for the faces of the larger models only three sizes of brushes are needed: No. 3, No. 0, and No. 00, No. 3 being for covering the mass areas, No. 0 for all medium work and No. 00 for all the very fine detail. The care of brushes cannot be over emphasised, a dirty brush can do a great deal of damage and entail you in a great deal of unnecessary work in obliterating very often almost finished work, so you have been warned. Brushes should be cleaned after the use of each colour in the thinners of the paint you are using. When finishing the painting session the brushes should then be washed with warm water and almost any good household soap, rinsing gently, allowing most of the soap to remain in the hairs of the brush then brought to a fine point by running it through your fingers. Before using the brush again on a further session of painting place it under some running warm water and rinse the soap free from the hairs.

Soldier models throughout the years have been painted in almost every paint that ever came on the market, and we still go on experimenting, such is the search for perfection. The generally accepted paints by the enthusiasts are oil paints and water-bound oil paints (for the larger figures I have used water-proof poster colours). Your model shop stockist can, I feel sure, recommend the most suitable and best paint available. Whatever you choose, or which-ever you are recommended to, the result must be in a flat finish. The shiny gloss paints must be reserved for the parts of the dress and equipment which are supposed to have a polished surface effect. There is a wide range of metallic paints to choose from for painting metal parts such as buttons, badges, buckles, parts of weapons, etc. With your paints selected, your brushes at hand and your model primed, the last precaution is to see that your paints are well and truly mixed, stirring deep down to the bottom of your tin or jar allowing the pigment to be mixed thoroughly with the binder and thinners.

A working palette of glass or porcelain, which is easily cleaned, I find most useful for mixing. Some wiping rags should always be at hand along with spare jars of thinners for cleaning the brushes; never clean a white or light colour in the same jar as the darker colours. Now to actually painting the model, first concentrate on the eye giving the primer a further coat of bluish-white over the whole of the socket area. Now with the No. oo brush paint in with either light blue or burnt sienna small circles in the centre of the eyeballs to represent the irises, making certain that these are absolutely equal in size and the same distance from the nose. With the same brush, mark in a black dot to form the pupil in the centre of the blue or brown circles and in direct line with the corners of the mouth. Mix some burnt sienna with just that touch of white and with this colour draw in the lower eyelids arching them slightly, cutting both the whites of the eyes and the top of the blue or brown circles. Study the finished eyes very carefully, any alteration must be done now before the flesh tone is applied. The eyes having passed your scrutiny, you now mix on your palette the basic flesh colours, these being white, burnt sienna and mid-yellow. With these colours blended together any shade of skin colouring can be made. As no two people seem to have the same skin colouring it is advisable never to use a ready mixed flesh tone, always mix the paints to suit your model. The mixture of the flesh tone is now painted on the face bringing the colour up to the eyes and just covering the eyelid lines. With the flesh colour paint in the hands. Whilst the flesh colour is still wet mix a little sienna with it on the palette, paint around the eyes, down the sides of the nose and under the bottom lip. Without allowing the face to dry out, mix a tinge of red with some flesh tone and with this reddish-flesh colour paint in just below the cheek bone and blend the colours in. Paint the same colour over the ear and paint in the mouth. Mark out between the fingers and around the cuffs where the sleeves and the hands

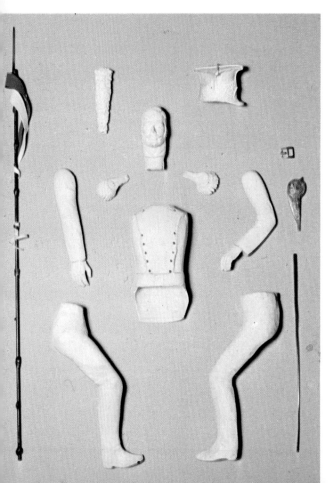

Upper.
Various heads ready for painting to fit the 30 cm models. Amongst these can be seen the castings of George V of England, the German Kaiser and a Prussian Hussar.

Lower.
A 30 cm model in parts made from the latex composition and an unmade metal sword and lance.

Right.
The latex composition models are shown here made in kit form. The author painting these 30 cm figures, is seen here giving his models of the Chasseur a Cheval an under-coating of waterproof paint, in preparation for applying the final colours. Each piece is painted before assembling, the equipment being added later.

meet. With a little deeper red apply to the upper lip and allow this to dry out. Using an undiluted burnt sienna, mark in the nostrils, the separation line between the lips and just the faintest application over the upper eyelid. For the smaller figures it is better to paint in the highlights, this is achieved by mixing white with the basic flesh colour and carefully applying to the cheeks, the ears, the nose, the chin and the hands. Eyebrows and hair can now be painted in the colour of your choice.

The painting of the uniform brings us on to the next stage. Here a dead matt paint is essential even to the extent of a further addition of matting agent to our paint to bring a feeling of texture to the material. Always try to work from the inside to the outside, by that I mean paint in the under garments first such as shirts, socks, etc., then fill in the trousers, gaiters, hessians, etc. These should be brought up to the finished state, then the outer clothes are painted and then finally the equipment, crossbelts, straps, pouches, etc. (pages 80 and 121). The shadows and highlights are now put on, the ideal way to give a depth to the folds and creases of the uniform is the following method. Mix a deeper tint of the basic colour by adding black or brown and paint into the shadow parts then, mixing the colour with a little more black or dark brown, line in the innermost part of the shadow area. Increase the depth of the folds by adding a highlight on the leading edge by adding white to the basic colour. With a brief study at your local museum of some of the old master oil-paintings you will discover many of the lighting tricks of light and shade, expecially on the clothes. Generally speaking, painting a horse is treated in the same manner as a figure with a white undercoat over-all. If any markings such as stars or blazes (page 102 upper) are required, these areas are given a further coat of white. The eye with the iris a dark brown has a black dot in the centre to indicate the pupil. Having decided on the final colour of the horse, colour the nostrils and the indentations of the muscles with a darker shade of the same colour. Where there are the thinner hair areas which are just in front of the hips on the flanks, on the lower breast between the legs and on the face around the eyes and the muzzle, these are painted in a lighter shade of the horse colouring. With these colours in a wet state the main colour is painted on, blending in the lights and the darks, giving an overall realistic effect of a well groomed horse. The mane of the horse should be lightly streaked with a lighter colour to give an alive flowing feeling about it. To complete the painting of the horse the legs can be finished with some sort of relief such as white socks or any of the other leg markings shown on the lower part of page 102. The horse reining and harness should be studied very carefully, especially the decorations of the brass work, etc. A finished model can be ruined by an incorrect harness. There are several good books on this subject, although most kits give most of the parts making the reining that much easier. The shabraques must also be studied with great care (page 110). The colours and regimental devices are most important and add greatly to the splendid authenticity of your models.

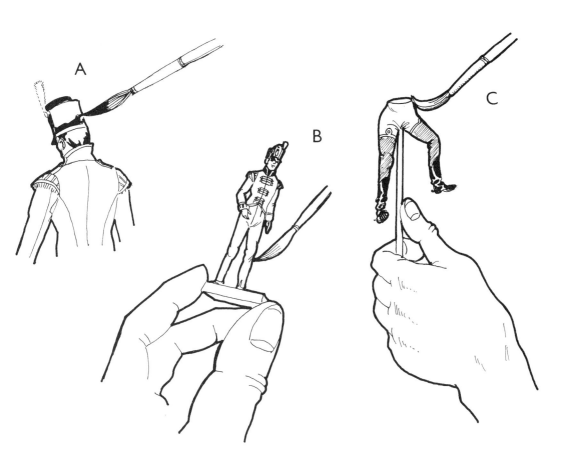

PAINTING A FIGURE (Fig. 21)

A. Painting the hat.
B. The whole uniform is painted and allowed to dry. The equipment which has already been painted is then attached.
C. A thin piece of dowel stick is inserted into the seat of the riding figure for easier painting. This can then be slipped into an empty bottle and allowed to dry off.

This shows the painting of the horse markings.
Upper. The head from left to right:—Strip, Star, Star and Strip, Star, Strip and Snip and Blaze.
Lower. The leg markings from left to right:—Coronet, Pastern, Fetlock, Sock and Stocking.

Right.
A 30 cm high model of a Polish Lancer of the Guard, the 1st Regiment of Napoleon's Bodyguard, carrying a metal sword and lance made from a latex composition. In 1807 they were the Polish Light Horse Regiment, becoming Lancers in 1809. After Napoleon's defeat in 1814, a body of Polish Lancers accompanied him to Elba. They were disbanded in 1815.

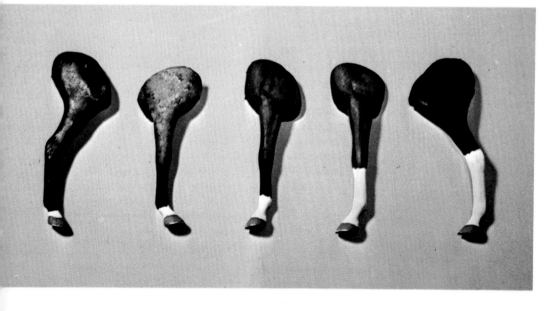

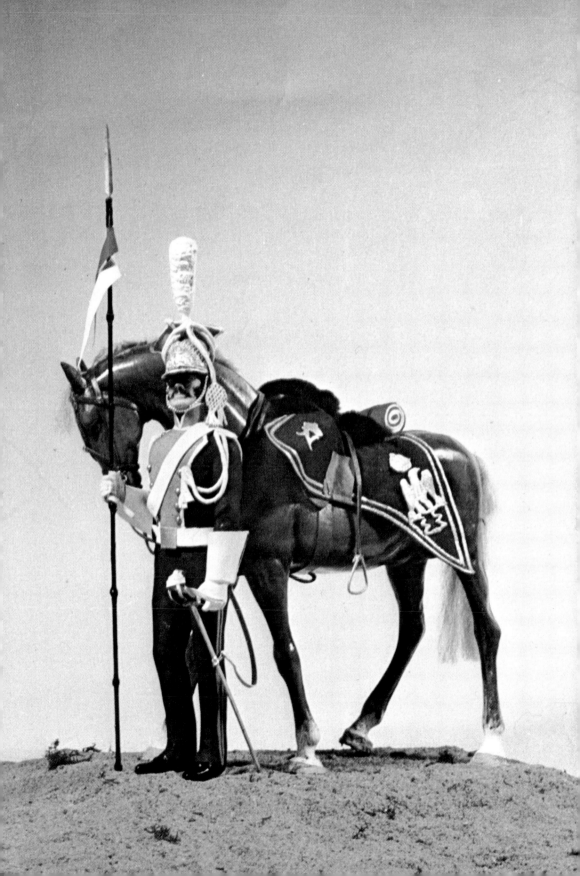

PAINTING A HORSE (Fig. 22)

Illustrated are a few examples of the markings of the horses.

A. Shown is a horse with a blaze down its nose.

B. A horse with a star in the centre between its eyes.

C. This shows a horse with a combined star and strip.

PAINTING THE FACE (Fig. 23)

1. The whole of the eye sockets are painted with a whitish blue.
2. The irises of the eyes are marked in making sure that these are both the the same size and equal distances apart from the nose.
3. The pupils of the eyes are now placed in the centre of the iris and in line with the corners of the mouth as shown in 'X'.
4. Mark in the upper and lower eyelids in a burnt sienna with the finest brush. Paint in close to the pupil and this will cut down the amount of white in the eye.
5. As instructed, mix up the flesh colour of yellow, white and burnt sienna to the correct consistency and tone, bringing the flesh colour to the eyes and blending the flesh tone with the burnt sienna surrounding the eyes. With this colour paint the hands of the model.
6. Before the flesh colour is completely dry, mix it with a little red and apply to the mouth and just under the cheeks, blending the cheek colour into the face. With the same colour outline the ears, under the jaw line and in between the fingers. Adding a little more red, mark in the upper lip and, with pure burnt sienna, mark in the nostrils and separation between the lips.
7. The eyebrows and hair are now added and the uniform is then painted.

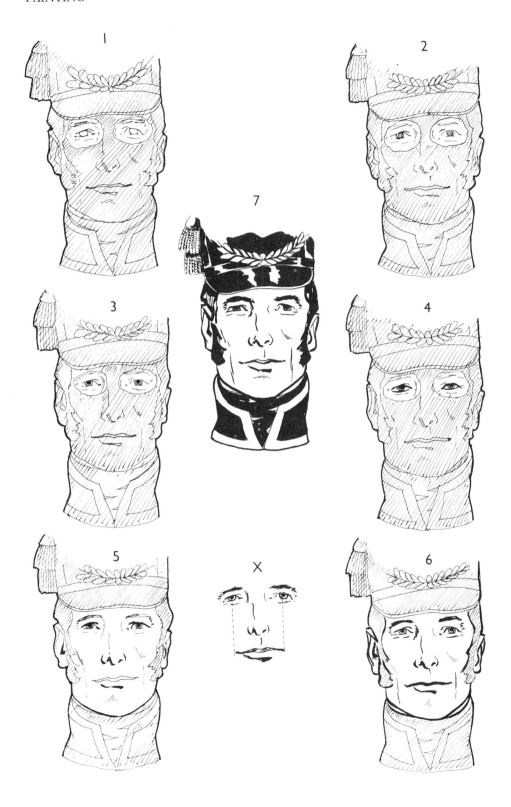

A British 10th Hussar of 1900 being made. The sabretache has not been fitted, the sword has yet to be added and the shabraque to be adjusted and finished. The figure stands 45 cm high and is made of a latex composition. The 10th became a Hussar Regiment on an order dated April 1811.

Horse and Harness

Now comes the question of the horse and harness. This seems to be the least discussed from the point of view of the model soldier enthusiast. Few model books give any great reference to that wonderful animal and the great part it played in the battles of yesteryear.

Knowing just the basic facts about the horse is sufficient for the enthusiast and there are many excellent non-military books on this subject which are included in the bibliography. The points of the horse and the method of measuring are given in Figure 24.

The cavalry of the past were not, as one would expect, very good horsemen and the control and training of the horses was achieved with a great deal of harshness, most European armies used the 'curb' bit. This was a piece of metal shaped into the figure 'H', the upright sides being called the 'branches' and in the centre was a bar with a shaped bend which varied considerably depending on the treatment given to the horse.

The bridle consisted of a crown piece which lay across the head just behind the ears and extended down on either side of the face of the horse. These extensions are called the cheek pieces. From just in front of the ears and attached on either side of the temple is the brow band. The cheek pieces support the nose-band and the bit which is held in the mouth of the horse. The hussar pattern of bridle had two extra straps which fastened cross-wise on the horse's face and was ornamented with a medallion. From the top of the cheek piece at the junction of the brow-band, a strap passed under the neck and fastened at the same point on the other side, this being known as the 'throat latch'. The control of the horse was achieved by a chain which was attached to the upper ring of the bit where the cheek straps were attached and which ran from either side under the horse's chin. Attached to the lower branch of the bit was a rein which is known as the 'curb rein' and by the rider pulling on this rein the U-shape on the bit turned and thrust the point or 'spade' of the U-shape into the roof of the horse's mouth. The second rein which was fastened on the upper branch of the bit was called the 'snaffle'.

It was quite common practice for the cheek pieces, which were attached to the nose-band, to be a different colour to the one which fastened to the bit. When assembling your kits, start with the strap holding any medallions or crescents; most hussar regiments had some form of ornamentation hanging from the throat latch. It was not uncommon for a cavalryman to also have a martingale. This was a strap which was fastened to the nose-band and to the saddle girth. Now place on the face pieces, the crown and cheek pieces, then the brow and nose bands.

The saddle should fit as close as possible to the back but leave a clearance of the withers and along the length of the backbone. The girth band is placed in the sternum curb which is just behind the elbows and is, to all intent and purpose, the horse's waistline. A crupper strap is also used to keep the saddle in position.

The shabraque is placed over the saddle and an additional girth strap is then fixed over and fastened to the saddle girth band. The cantel of the saddle comes through the aperture which is cut away on the shabraque. Sheep skins, if worn, are fastened on by straps around the pummel and the cantel of the saddle. Finally the portmanteaux and blankets are attached just behind the cantel.

POINTS OF THE HORSE (Fig. 24)

1. Muzzle.
2. Salt cellar.
3. Forelock.
4. Nape.
5. Crest.
6. Mane.
7. Withers.
8. Back.
9. Loins.
10. Croup.
11. Dock or crupper.
12. Buttock.
13. Quarters.
14. Gaskin.
15. Point of the hock.
16. Ergot or fetlock.
17. Hoof.
18. Coronet.
19. Pastern.
20. Hind cannon bone.
21. Chestnut.
22. Stifle.
23. Flank.
24. Point of the hip.
25. Back of ribs.
26. Belly.
27. Point of elbow.
28. Forearm.
29. Knee.
30. Breast.
31. Shoulder.
32. Point of shoulder.
33. Neck.
34. Cheek.

A horse is measured in hands, which is about 10 cm. This measurement is taken from ground level to the peak of the withers (number 7 on the chart of 'points of the horse').

A. B. C. The bridle consists of the crown pieces, brow bands, cheek pieces, nose bands, face straps, throat latch with a crescent medallion, curb rein, snaffle reins, leather halter and martingale.

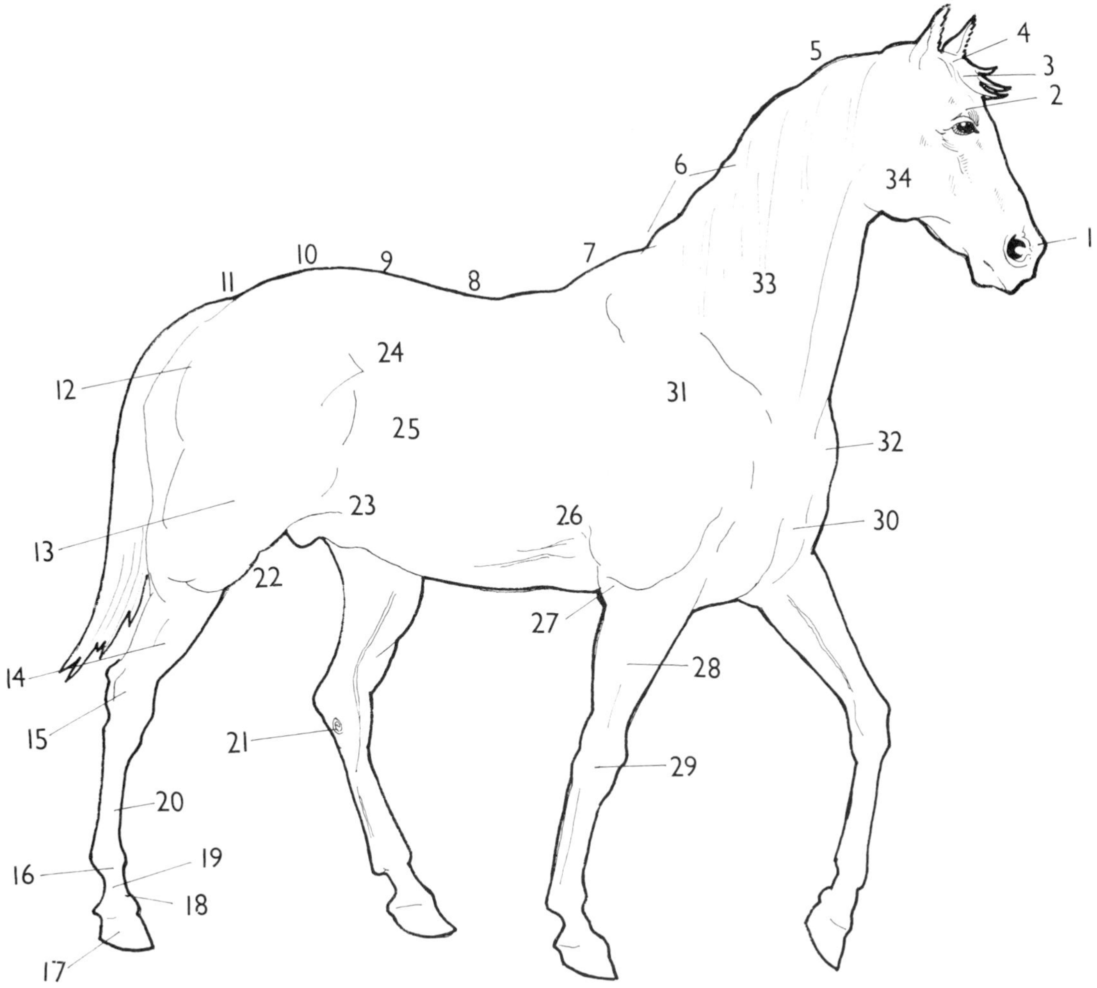
1
2
3
4
5
6
7
8
9
10
11
12
13
14
15
16
17
18
19
20
21
22
23
24
25
26
27
28
29
30
31
32
33
34

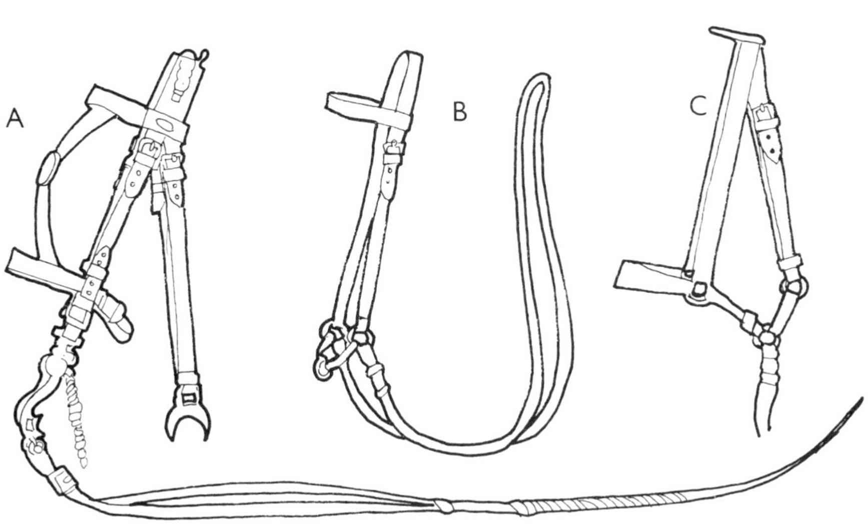
A
B
C

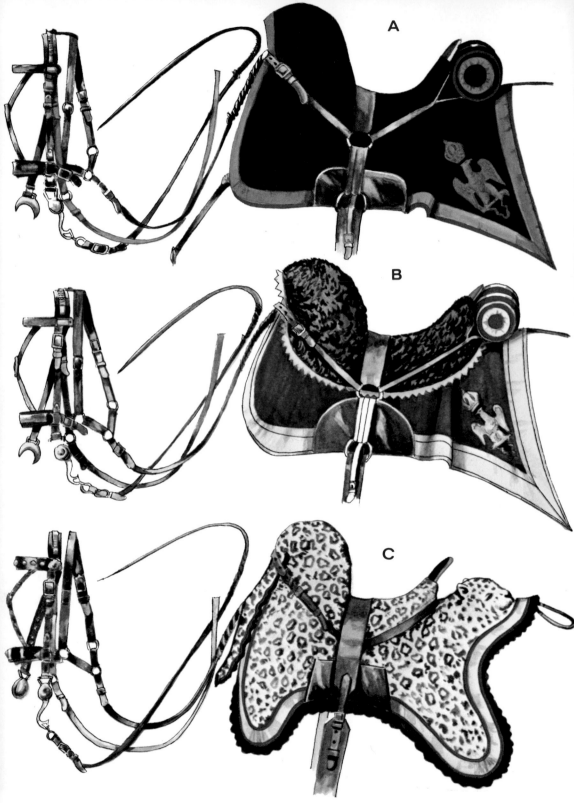

Illustrations of three types of French saddles and shabraques with harness of a browband, headpieces, throat straps, cheek pieces, nose bands, bits, snaffle reins, curb reins and girth, etc.
A. Chasseur a Cheval. B. Lancer Regiment. C. Officer's whole leopard skin shabraque of the Chasseur a Cheval of the Guard.

A 45 cm high figure of a British Hussar of the 11th Hussar Regiment which is made in a latex composition. This model depicts an Officer dressed in battle order during the Crimean War of 1854. They formed part of the famous Light Cavalry Brigade during the heroic charge on the Russian guns at Balaclava which although an impossible task showed great courage.

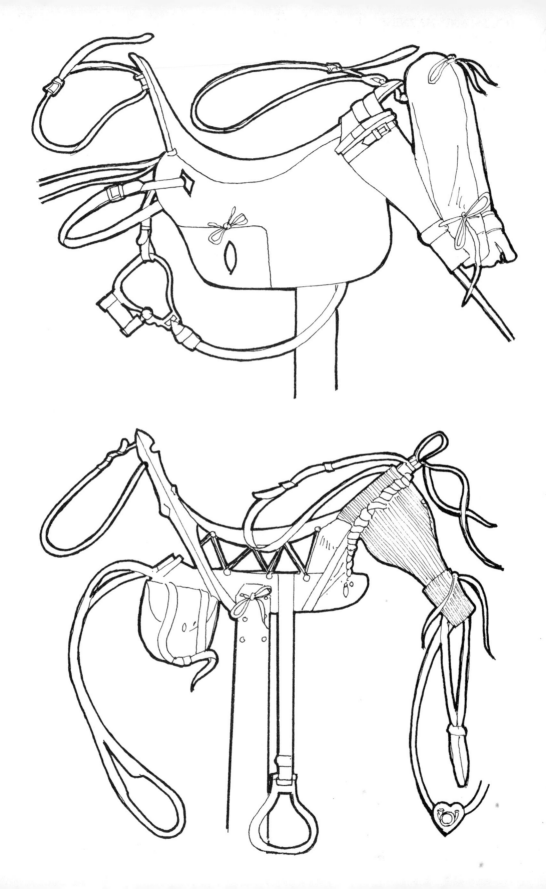

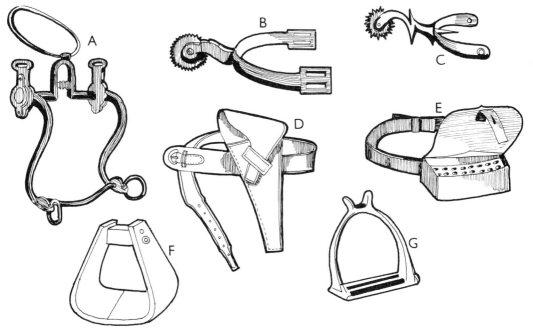

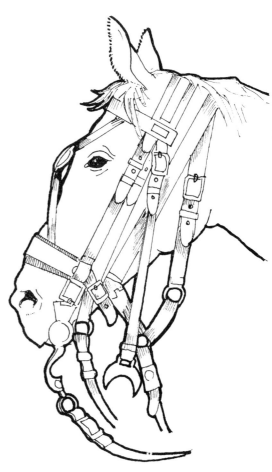

LANCER SADDLE (Fig. 25)
left upper

This Lancer saddle is not unlike the Hussar saddle with the deep dip in the seat and the high arches. The high narrow 'spoon' rose from the centre of the cantle allowing a great deal of perhaps unnecessary baggage to be carried. This type of saddle was adopted throughout Europe and the Americas.

HUSSAR SADDLE (Fig. 26)
Left lower

The tree of the Hussar saddle is shown here as adopted from the Hungarians. Due to lacing the gaps between the side-bars with rawhide, which was then stretched very tightly, the space along the spine of the horse was left completely free from the weight of the rider. The deep seat allowed the horseman to sit comfortably into the saddle.

HARNESS ACCESSORIES (Fig. 27)

A. Bronzed U.S. bit with ring. B. A strap spur. C. Screw-out neck spur. D. Pistol belt of patent leather. E. Cartridge-box. F. Stirrup used by the U.S. Cavalry, 1860. G. A stirrup as used by the Confederate Army, 1860.

FULL HEAD HARNESS (Fig. 28)
Right

The horse illustrated has the full head harness of a Hussar Regiment. Here can clearly be seen the crown band, brow band, cheek pieces, the face crossed straps with the medallion, the nose band, the throat latch, the martingale, the snaffle and curb reins.

A superb 54 mm metal kit assembly model of Winston Churchill as a young man, entitled 'Young Winston' at Omdurman, 1898 and made by PHOENIX MODEL DEVELOPMENTS LTD. Sir Winston Churchill was born at Blenheim Palace on 30th November 1874. He was Prime Minister of England in 1940 and again in 1951. He was knighted in 1953 and died on 24th January 1965.

Left.
A 45 cm latex composition model of a mounted British Life Guard Officer. Apart from a few minor details the uniform of the Household Cavalry has remained unchanged since the middle of the nineteenth century. An Officer wears an aiguilette on the right shoulder showing that he is one of the Queen's personal bodyguard. When in action they are an armoured car regiment.

REINS (Fig. 29)

A. The pull on all four reins with the left hand.
  a. The off-snaffle rein.
  b. The near-snaffle rein.
  c. The off-curb rein.
  d. The near-curb rein.
  e. The end of the snaffle reins.
  f. The end of the curb reins.

B. The position of the curb rein in use.
  a. The off-curb rein.
  b. The near-curb rein.
  c. The off-snaffle rein.
  d. The near-snaffle rein.
  e. The end of the curb reins.
  f. The end of the snaffle reins.

C. With the knuckles of the hand in the low position showing the use of the curb rein.
  a. The off-snaffle rein.
  b. The near-snaffle rein.
  c. The off-curb rein.
  d. The near-curb rein.
  e. The end of the curb reins.
  f. The end of the snaffle reins.

D. With the knuckles raised showing the pull of the near curb rein.
  a. The near-snaffle rein.
  b. The off-snaffle rein.
  c. The near-curb rein.
  d. The off-curb rein.
  e. The end of the curb reins.
  f. The end of the snaffle reins.

E. Showing the separating of the reins.
  a. The off-snaffle rein.
  b. The near-snaffle rein.
  c. The off-curb rein.
  d. The near-curb rein.
  e. The end of the snaffle reins.
  f. The end of the curb reins.

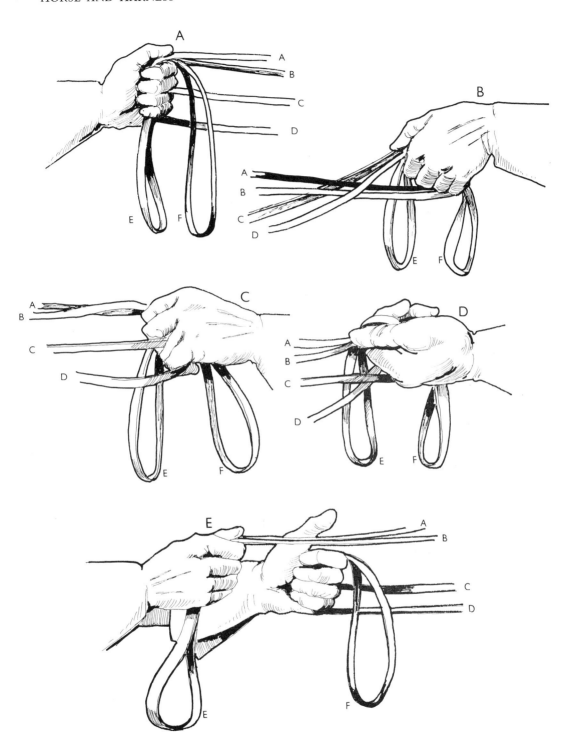

A

B

C

D

E

See page 120 for caption

Captions for pages 118 and 119

Model of a Chasseur à Cheval in the making. The mounted Chasseur is being dressed in the escort service dress. The horse is unpainted and without its mane and tail, and has no harness. This famous regiment first saw service as guides formed by the General Bonaparte for his Italian Campaign in 1796.

A reference illustration of a Chasseur à Cheval of the Guard.
A. Sword belt with bayonet, sabre and sabretache.
B. Chasseur in full dress as worn on service escort duty, 1805–14.
C. Chasseur's dolman.
D. Chasseur's pelisse.
E. Chasseur's colpack complete with flounders, tassels and plume.
The first company of Chasseurs à Cheval was formed on the 3rd January 1800.

CUIRASSIER 9th Regiment 1812 (Fig. 30)

A. A mounted cuirassier of the 9th Regiment of about 1812. The shabraque was dark blue cloth edged in white. The regimental number, in white, was placed on the ends of the portmanteau behind the saddle. An embroidered grenade was placed in the corner of the shabraque, sometimes the number of the regiment also appeared here. The shabraque and pistol covers were in red cloth with a dark green serrated border edged in gold. Only the troopers carried a portmanteau behind the saddle. The harness was black leather with brass fittings. The horse is seen here in the trot position.

B. An Officer of the Saxon Chevau Legers of 1812. The shabraque was in red cloth with a dark green serrated border edged in gold.

C. A horse fitted with a halter.

D. A trooper of the Grenadier à Cheval de la Garde 1804–1815. The shabraque and pistol covers were in dark blue edged with a wide yellow border. An embroidered yellow crown was placed in the lower back corner of the shabraque. The horse is seen in the trotting position.

E. An angle of the hoof which presents an important action in the horse movements.

A French Captain of the Chasseurs a Cheval of the Guard in service dress, 1812–15, made by HISTOREX in plastic and stands 54 mm high. The Chasseurs were the Emperor's nearest Guard, and when he went on campaign they always provided his escort. In 1815, on the Emperor's return from exile in Elba, they were reformed as the 2nd Regiment of the Chasseurs a Cheval of the Young Guard.

Left.
The author placing a 30 cm model of the Chasseur a Cheval in position in front of the mounted Chasseur. The model, mounted, stands 45 cm high. On 14th November 1801 the Chasseurs became a regiment. In 1804 they became the Garde Imperiale, and Napoleon wore the undress uniform of his Chasseurs on most occasions.

Dioramas

The display of models is a combination of the detailed perfection of the model soldiers coupled with an authentic looking background which together tell a story of an action long since past but, to the collector, a captured moment in time. With just two or three figures any collector can also tell a story or part of a story. Depending on the size of the diarama within any limited area, it is possible to make a diarama so that at all times it can be improved upon and extended so that each scene becomes just a piece in a very large jigsaw. There must, therefore, be some prior planning to allow for each piece to become an action within itself and which in turn will become part of a greater action, until eventually a whole battle scene is completed. An impossible dream? Certainly not, each collector has the ability to achieve this. The idea is a simple one. Each base must be shaped according to the set plan and a simple locking piece fitted which will find a corresponding locking piece in the next scene. For each scene or diarama take a piece of wood of 12 mm thickness, cut to shape according to the master plan and fit struts underneath to prevent warping. The surface is then covered with very small tacks which in turn are hammered in and then lightly bent over. This will be the 'key' to hold the papier maché pulp which will completely cover the diarama base. The pulp, when made, is the most inexpensive form of modelling composition which can form the perfect earth terrain contours and is the ideal building material for walls, rocks, cobblestones, dirt roads and parade-ground surfaces. The pulp is very easy to make, simply soak torn pieces of newspaper in a bowl of warm water (the soaking should be as long as possible, preferably overnight) and then rub between the hands to a pulpy condition. The pulp should be put through an ordinary household mincing machine if one is available, as this will break up the pulp to a finer consistency. Form the pulp into a bowl shape and pour in some hot liquid glue size which is then mixed together. The mixture is again formed into the bowl shape and this time dry plaster of Paris powder is added and mixed. The mixture is now very malleable, a modelling composition which can be spread over the surface of the wooden base and shaped into the surface texture of the terrain required. The models, when arranged in their respective positions, should be pressed firmly into the pulp composition. This will hold them very fast when dry. Added textures can be sprinkled over the surface whilst still wet and when it is dry, may be painted over with almost any type of paint using of course, all earth colours. Over these, whilst still wet, can be strewn coloured sawdust and sand. If a snow scene is required, a light paint over with white and then a sprinkle of white glitter will do the trick. This will adhere to both the wet paint and the pulp. With our pulp mixture hills and rocks can be built with the simplest foundations. Water effects can quite easily be built within the composition, either with glass or a clear liquid plastic. Within a few days the whole diarama will be dry and will then form a solid construction. Once the terrain surface has been formed on the baseboard, the rocks, tracks and streams are marked in. The task of smoothing in the terrain is a simple procedure of modelling with the use of a small glass of water and either a modelling spatula or the modeller's best friend, the fingers. Ruts can be made by running a gun or vehicle which is to be used in the diarama through the pulp mixture then wiped clean again with a soft tissue without any ill effects. Trees are formed by either covering a 12 mm diameter dowel stick with small tacks or wrapping the dowel around with wire. The papier maché pulp is laid on with a modelling tool, the bark effect is traced over the surface. The branches are twisted wire pieces extending from the main stem of the dowel and are in turn covered with the pulp and modelled with the same effect as the tree. When dry and given coats of brown and green the effect is very good. Rooftiles and cracked and broken walls showing shell and bullet holes look very effective when treated in the modelling method, as also do the fences which are made from balsa wood. Water effect is best achieved when made from the clear liquid plastic which can now be purchased from most Do-it-Yourself shops. (This is the same liquid plastic which is also used in the rubber moulds and can be cut and animated by gluing much the same as a lead figure.) If houses, buildings and sheds are used they should be built to last and it is therefore advisable to spend some time and effort to achieve this end. The frames are faced with a thin hardboard which is covered with a thin layer of pulp mixture and marked out with a modelling tool. Frames should be made for the roof sections and then covered with a 'peg-board' hardboard over which the pulp mixture is sprinkled and the tiles modelled on. No great skill is required and most efforts when painted look very professional. Books on older architectural buildings are a great asset if the action of the diarama calls for certain periods when the battle was fought within a city, town, or village. There is nothing like authenticity to improve and put the finishing touches to your scene.

A German Anti-Aircraft gun and crew in action in a day and night diarama scene made by ELASTOLIN of Germany c. 1939. This diarama shows the effect of how special lighting photography can emphasise different aspects of the same group, making quite a dramatic alteration from a day to a night scene.

The simple diarama, now in a finished form, is composed with HISTOREX models of British, Prussian and Spanish Hussars. The camera captures the desolate atmosphere of the aftermath of a battleground showing the variations on a scene seen by night and day.

MAKING A DIORAMA (Figs. 31 and 32)

A. Cutting the joints for the transverse pieces of the frame.

B. Drilling and fixing the base board to the frame.

C. Hammering in the tacks.

D. Preparing the paper in the water by tearing it into small pieces.

E. Feeding the mincing machine with the wet and torn pieces of paper.

F. Pouring the hot glue size into the paper pulp, then mixing together throughly.

G. Adding the plaster of Paris to the glue and paper pulp, resulting in a malleable papier maché pulp.

H. On the left a small trowel for laying on the pulp mixture. On the right a metal plaster rasp, ideal for roughing up the ground texture and this tool will not clog up.

I. Wire-ended model tools ideal for making the various diorama subjects.

J. Laying on the papier maché pulp, using oddments of wood, cardboard, etc., to help build up the mounds and folds of the terrain.

K. A small pool scooped out of the mixture and a tree being 'planted' into position.

L. The bark of the tree being modelled on to the dowel stick which is covered with wire.

M. A farmhouse framed out.

N. This shows the joints of the frames.

O. The framing of part of the outhouse and the facing treated with papier maché pulp.

P. The framing of the window piece, also with its facing treated with papier maché pulp.

A

B

C

D

E

F

G

H

I

Illustrating simple diarama building. This diarama is made on a wooden base covered with papier mache pulp, which is an ideal cheap material for modelling earth contours, backed up with plasticine and plaster, glue, sand and various coloured sawdusts and finally paint.

2nd LANCERS OF THE IMPERIAL GUARD (Fig. 33)

A. A lancer complete in review order wearing the traditional Polish head-dress called a chapka. The coatee or kurta was of red cloth. The cross belt, waist belt, sword knot and sling were of white leather, with brass fittings. The pouch was in black leather. On the waist belt was a rect-angular brass plate bearing the Imperial eagle with a crown above it. The overalls were also of red cloth with a double broad blue stripe down the outer seam. Gauntlet gloves were worn.

B. Front view of the chapka without a plume. The hat had a black leather body and peak. The square top was covered in red cloth and edged in yellow with twisted cords and tassels, also in yellow cord. The brassrayed chapka plate had a white metal centre with the letter 'N' in brass. The chin scales were of brass. On the left hand top was the tri-colour cockade.

C. Front view of the kurta which was of red cloth with a dark blue plastron, collar, cuffs and turnbacks. (This could be turned back to reveal an all-red front.) All the seams were piped in blue, the epaulette had a yellow fringe and the aiguilettes which hung on the left side were of yellow cord. All the buttons were brass.

D. The tri-colour cockade.

E. Epaulette was bound in dark blue on the upper side with a yellow fringe.

F. Back view of the kurta showing the seam lines which were piped in dark blue. The collar, cuffs, turnbacks and belt loop were also in dark blue.

G. Side view of the chapka showing the yellow flounders and tassels and hat cords which joined on the left side, from which issued a large white plume.

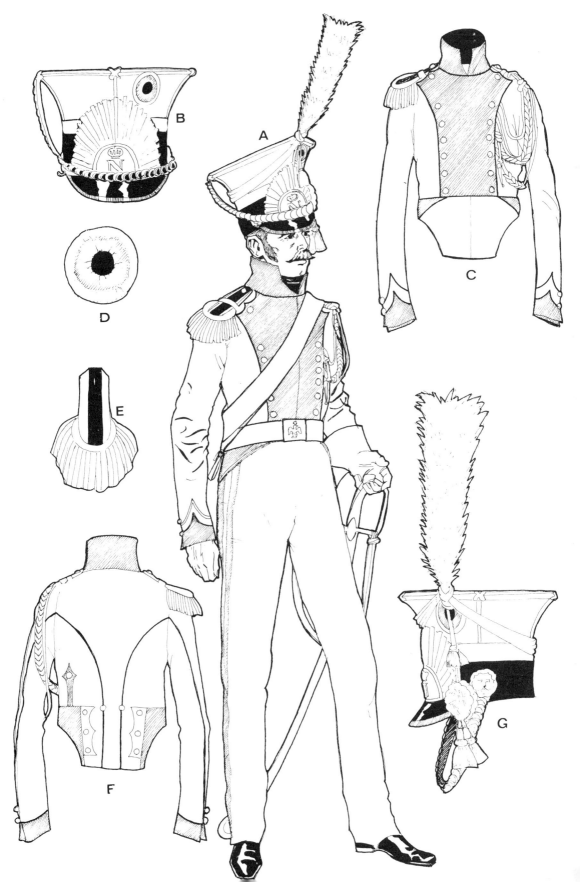

A

B

C

D

E

F

G

Right.
A 30 cm model of an American paratrooper of 1944 in a latex composition. These specialised troops had constant changes due to experience gained under battle conditions.

Above.
30 cm models in a latex composition of an American paratrooper in the 1944 period. One picture shows American, British and German paratroopers. As can be seen from these pictures, the full equipment worn by the American paratrooper included the 'Mae West' and the reserve parachute in the front.

FRENCH CUIRASSIER 1812 (Fig. 34)

A. Figure of a trooper of the Regiment of Cuirassiers of France *c.* 1812. The short-tailed coatee was dark blue, with the collars, cuffs and turn-backs in the facing colours;

1st, 2nd, 3rd	—Red
4th, 5th, 6th	Orange
7th, 8th, 9th	—Yellow
10th, 11th, 12th	—Rose.

The turnbacks were embroidered with a grenade device. Red epaulettes with red fringes were worn by all cuirassier regiments. The buff breeches were worn with high knee stockings and high black boots. White gauntlet gloves were worn.

B. The sword belt, sword knot, slings and bayonet frog were in white leather with brass buckles and fittings. The heavy duty straight steel sabre had a brass three barred hilt.

C. The helmet had a steel body and peak around which was a band of fur. The brass crest had at the front a black short tuft of hair and from the top a fall of black horse hair. A black plume was worn, but only in review order. The bosses and chin scales were of brass.

D. A cavalry type pistol, mark AN IX.

E. The pouch and carbine belt were in white leather with brass buckle and fittings. The pouch was in black leather.

F. The two piece cuirass, which covered the chest and back, was of steel with brass buttons around the edge. The lining was of red cloth, piped in white. The clasps which fastened the cuirass were made of brass scales. A leather belt joined the cuirass at the waist.

G A cavalry pistol mark AN XIII.

H. A carbine musket mark AN IX.

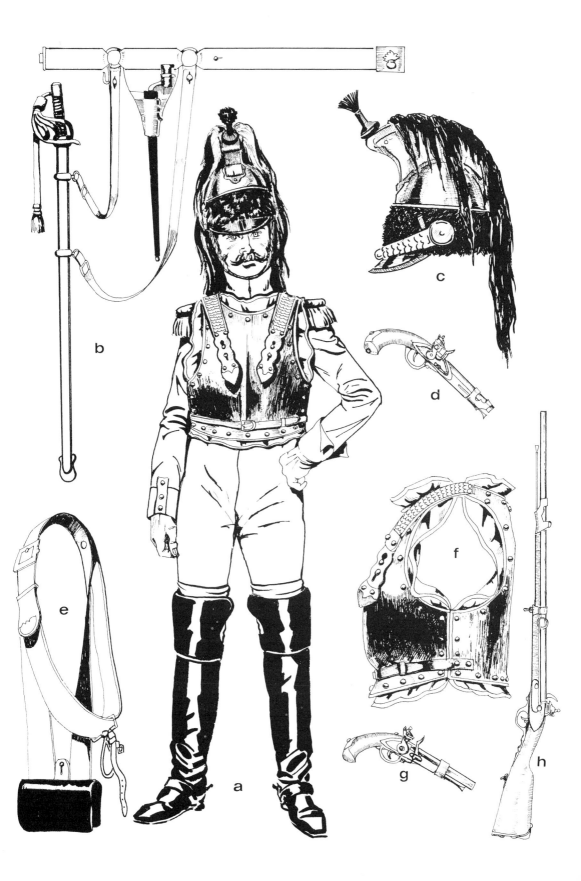

30 cm model in latex composition of a German paratrooper of the 1942–44 period. In one picture he is shown meeting Field Marshal Rommel. A Fallschirmjager (as the German paratroopers were called) is seen here wearing his 'knochensack', the popular name of the jump-suit. The four views give a good idea of the equipment he carried at that period.

30 cm models of British paratroopers, c. 1944. One picture shows a British and German paratrooper. They are made of a latex composition. The British paratrooper is wearing the smock and is equipped with ammunition pouches and the famous 'Sten' automatic gun.

SOME IMPORTANT TOOLS AND EQUIPMENT REQUIRED

Balsa wood.
Epoxy adhesive.
Evostick.
Polystyrene glue.
Thin metal sheets.
Lead.
Cold set solder.
Straight pins, various sizes.
Thread.
Fine guage fuse wire.
Craft knife and assorted blades.
Pencil-type soldering iron.
Razor saw.
Small set square.
Steel ruler.
Scriber or engraver.
Small vice.
Sharpening stone.
Nails.
Tacks.
Rasps.
Turpentine or paint thinners.
Plaster of Paris.
Mixing bowl.
Latex composition
Paint brushes 000 to 3.
Square aluminium wire.
Knitting needle.
Vinamold.
Liquid detergent.
Graphite powder.
Paints, water based and enamel.
Small jars or tins.
Rags for wiping.
Figure iron.

Water jug.
Wire-ended modelling tools.
Wood and metal spatulas.
Plaster rasp.
Small trowel.
Block of metal.
Small hammer.
Long-nosed pliers.
Tweezers.
Needle files.
Razor blades.
Sandpaper, fine to flour.
Scissors.
Soldering iron.
Solder.
Wire cutters.
X-Acto knife.
Fine saw.
Watchmakers screwdriver.
Clay.
Plasticine.
Low melt metal alloy.
Liquid plastic and catalyst.
Cold cure silicone rubber compound.
Fine chain.
Metal tubing, small diameter.
Dowel sticks in various sizes.
Sailmakers needles.
Wooden mixing spoon.
Glue size.
Wood for bases.
Pencils.
Palette of glass or porcelain.
Dividers.

Glossary

Aiguillette	shoulder strap of cord with a decorative knot and loops of plain or plaited cords fastening to a button
Armature wire	wire used for forming the skeleton structure used to build clay models
Austrian knot	similar to Hungarian knot, an ornamental cord design worn on cuffs and the front of trousers
Bandolier	wide belt on which powder flasks and cartridge pouches were carried
Barrel belt	a belt worn by hussar regiments, encircles the waist and ends in tassels
Baton	ornamental military stick carried by officers
Bearskin	large bearskin head-dress of fur worn by grenadiers
Bicorne	a two-pointed hat with the points usually to the front and back
Bonnet de Police	the name used for a French soldier's forage or fatigue cap
Brandenburgs	decorative lace or cord linking two buttons
Breeches	tight fitting trousers
Brown Bess	the standard British musket from 1730 until the beginning of the nineteenth century
Burnous	cloak with sleeves of varying lengths and a hood
Busby	fur head-dress, smaller than a bearskin, worn by hussars, usually with a cloth bag falling to one side
Cap	soft head-dress of varying shapes, sometimes with a peak
Carbine	a short musket used mainly by cavalry
Cartouche	a small pouche worn on the shoulder belt
Chevrons	lace denoting rank
Chin scales	metal scales on a leather backing, fastened from the helmet and tied under the chin
Cockade	a rosette in the national colours of the country
Colpack	a round fur busby, often with a flap at the top hanging down one side
Contra-epaulette	epaulette without fringes

Diarama with model vehicles. A working model of the Honest John missile launcher, made by DINKY TOYS, model 665.

An example of how toys can create a realistic appearance as this fully working model of a bridge-laying vehicle shows on the left in this diarama, made by French DINKY TOYS, model 883. On the right is the Berliet Aurochs load carrier which comes complete with two skin divers, made by SOLIDO of France.

A Volkswagen KDF with a 50 mm P.A.K. anti-tank gun which can be detached and set in the firing position, made by DINKY TOYS, model 617.

A realistic plastic kit of the Panzer Kampfwagen LL Ausf. F/G which comes complete with five finely detailed figures of the Tank Commander, Infantry Officer and three foot soldiers. The models shown are assembled but un-painted. They are made by the Japanese firm of TAMIYA. The scale is 1/35th.

Lower. This equally fine model of a Horsch' Staff Car complete with three Officers and a driver was made by ELASTOLIN. The figures were made of a plaster composition and stood 7 cm high.

Cross belts	worn to carry the cartridge pouch, ammunition pouch, bayonet and sword
Cutaway	kind of tail coat with the fronts curving away slightly
Dolman	hussar type tight-fitting jacket
Epaulette	shoulder strap with fringes
Facings	parts of a uniform such as collar, cuffs and lapels which are in the colours of the regiment, different from the main colour of the uniform
Figure iron	iron support for building models
Flintlock	type of musket of which the lock had a flint
Flounders	flat, oval woven decorations usually hanging from the hat or shoulder
Fob	chain suspended from the waist, which carried the seal or a watch
Frock coat	originated in the eighteenth century for informal wear, eventually became the undress uniform
Gaiters	a covering cloth or leather for the ankles and lower legs. Fastened mainly at the side
Gauntlets	gloves with stiffened tops
'Hanger' sword	a short sword carried by the infantry
Hungarian knot	intricate braiding of interwoven circles on the thighs of hussar type breeches
Hussar boots	made of soft leather curving up at the front and back with a 'V' notch with sometimes a tassel at the front
Khaki	from the Persian word meaning dust or ashes
Kurta	loose-type blouse, reaching the knees, with an opening at the front to the waist
Lance	long wooden shaft with a pointed steel head from 3 to 5·5 metres long, often carrying a pennant at the head
Mirliton	tall cone-shaped peakless head-dress with a spiral wound round
Mitre	stiffened hat rising to a peak, often richly embroidered
Overalls	long trousers with a strap under the boots
Pelisse	fur-trimmed coatee worn by hussars, usually slung over the left shoulder

Pectoral	decorative part of a horse harness
Pickelhaube	German spiked helmet
Pickers	small pins used to clean the touch-hole of a firearm
Piping	raised edge around the collar, cuffs, jacket, pockets, seams, etc.
Plastron	front of a uniform, sometimes fastened back to display the facing colours
Pom-pom	a round worsted wool ball worn on headgear in place of a plume
Riding breeches	breeches with extra width given over the thighs, giving them their characteristic shape
Sabre	sword with curved blade
Sabretache	plain or embroidered flat bag attached by two or three slings to the sword belt
Sam Browne belt	used to support the sword from a waistbelt, named after General Sir Samuel Browne
Sash	band of material worn from right shoulder to left hip, or around the waist with hanging or tasseled ends either at the back or side
Shako	a peaked rigid head-dress either cylindrical or bell-topped
Shoulder straps	cloth shoulder pieces fastening near the collar, originally meant for keeping shoulder belts from slipping
Slash	cuff or coat ornamentation, usually with buttons
Spatula	flat wooden or metal modelling tool
Sword knot	strap worn around the wrist to the hilt of the sword to prevent its loss in action
Tricorne	a three-pointed hat replaced by a bicorne towards the end of the eighteenth century
Turban	Persian word meaning veil material from which the Persians made the tightly-tied close-fitting head-dress. The Arabs and other Eastern countries also adopted the turban
Turnbacks	tails of the coat folded and fastened back to reveal the lining or facing colour. Later they became sham and were sewn into place, being purely ornamental

A HISTOREX model of a British Hussar trooper of the 7th Regiment. 1812–15, 54 mm high, this model comes in a plastic kit form. On the 18th April 1811, the 7th Light Dragoon Regiment was converted to a Hussar Regiment, following the pattern of the Hungarian Light Cavalry. Although the uniform changed, the title remained for many years as Light Dragoon.

An assembled and painted Spanish Hussar of the Maria Luisa Regiment of the 1808 period is made by HISTOREX and in the 54 mm range. These figures are made in polystyrene or hard plastic. The detail is of the highest quality. The series cover soldiers of the Napoleonic era. The choice of position is offered with each kit, as there are alternative parts, e.g. arms, legs etc. which can also be purchased as separate items.

SOME BOOKS FOR FURTHER RESEARCH

Military Miniatures by P. Blum. Publisher: P. Hamlyn.

Model Soldiers by J. G Garratt. Publisher: Seeley Service.

Model Soldiers by H. Harris. Publisher: Octopus Books.

Old British Model Soldiers by L. W. Richards. Publisher: Arms and Armour Press.

Model Soldier Guide by C. A. Risley and W. F. Imrie. Publisher: Risley & Imrie.

Little Wars by F. Palmer. Publisher: Arms and Armour Press.

How to go Advanced Plastic Modelling by G. Ellis. Publisher: Patrick Stephens.

Military Models by P. Blum. Publisher: Odessy Press.

Armies of India by Lovett and McMunn. Publisher: A. and C. Black.

Little Wars by H. G. Wells. Publisher: Arms and Armour Press.

European Military Uniforms by P. Martin. Publisher: Spring Books.

Soldiers, Soldiers, Soldiers by R. Bowood. Publisher: P. Hamlyn.

Model Soldiers by W. Y. Carman. Publisher: Arms and Armour Press.

A History of the British Army (4 Vols.) by C. C. P. Lawson. Publisher: Norman Military Publications.

British Military Uniforms by W. Y. Carman. Publisher: Leonard Hill.

History of the Regiments and Uniforms of the British Army by R. M. Barnes.

History of the Scottish Regiments, by R. M. Barnes.

Military Uniforms of Britain and the Empire by R. M. Barnes.

Soldiers of London by R. M. Barnes.

(All R. M. Barnes books published by Seeley Service).

Mounted Troops of The British Army by Col. H. C. B. Rogers. Publisher: Seeley Service.

Indian Army Uniforms (Cavalry and Infantry, 2 Vols.) by W. Y. Carman. Publisher: Morgan-Grampian.

Military Uniforms of the World by P. Kannik. Publisher: Blandford Press.

Cavalry Uniforms by R. & C. Wilkinson-Latham. Publisher: Blandford Press.

Infantry Uniforms (2 Vols.) by R. & C. Wilkinson Latham. Publisher: Blandford Press.

Great Regiments by V. Melagari. Publisher: Wiedenfeld and Nicholson.

War Games by D. Featherstone. Publisher: Stanley Paul.

World Uniforms in Colour (2 Vols.) Publisher: Paul Stephens.

Great Military Battles edited by C. Falls. Publisher: Wiedenfeld and Nicholson.

European Military Uniforms by P. Martin. Publisher: P. Hamlyn.

Der Standhafte Zinnsoldat by P. Martin. Publisher: W. Keller & Co.

Handbuch der Uniformkunde by Knotel-Sieg. Publisher: Helmut Gerhard Schulz.

Unter Osterreichs Fahnen by H. V. Patera. Publisher: Verlag Styria, Vienna.

Formations und Uniformierungsgesch, by Pietsch. Publisher: Helmut Gerhard Schulz.

Dix siècles de Costume Militaire by H. Lachouque. Publisher: Hachette.

L'Uniforme et les Armes des Soldats du premier Empire (2 Vols.) by L. and F. Funken. Publisher: Casterman.

L'Uniforme et les Armes des Soldats de la Guerre 1914–18 (2 Vols.) by L. and F. Funken. Publisher: Casterman.

Le Costume et les Armes des Soldats de Tous les Temps (2 Vols.) by L. and F. Funken. Publisher: Casterman.

De la Cuirasse à la Tunique by H. Schneider. Publisher: Huber, Frauenfeld.

Zolnierz Polski by Bronislaw Gembarzewski. Publisher: Wydawnictwo Ministerstwa Obrony Narodowej Waszawa.

Hugh Evelyn Military series.

Almark books on Military subjects.

Osprey 'Men at Arms' series.

'Discovering' books. Publisher: Shire publications.
  Artillery.
  British Cavalry Regiments.
  British Military Badges and Buttons.
  British Military Uniforms.
  Edged Weapons.
  Famous Battles (2 Vols.).
  Militaria.
  Model Soldiers.
  Modelling for Wargamers.
Armour and Weapons by Foulkes. Publisher: Oxford University Press.

Book of the Horse by Sidney. Publisher: Cassell.

Fighting Men by Treece. Publisher: Brockhampton.

Handbook for Military Artificers. Publisher: H.M.S.O.

Horses and Saddlery by G. Tylden. Publisher: J. A. Allen & Co.

Horses of the World by Goodall. Publisher: Country Life.

Ordnance—The History of Army Ordnance Services by Forbes. Publisher: Medici Society.

Points of the Horse by Hayes. Publisher: Stanley Paul.

White Stallions of Vienna by Podhajsky. Publisher: Harrap.

MODEL SOLDIERS ON EXHIBITION

Belgium: Musée Royal de l'Armée, Brussels.
    Musée Gruuthuse, Bruges.

France: Inter-Allied Museum, Arromanches.
    Musée de l'Armée, Paris.
    Miniature Figurines Museum, Compiègne.
    Musée de la Marine, Paris.
    Historical Museum, Strasbourg.

Germany: Bayerisches National Museum, Munich.
    Germanisches Museum, Nuremberg.
    Deutches Zinnfigurenmuseum, Plassenburg Castle, Kulmbach.
    Hersbruck Museum, Nuremberg.

Italy: Museo Civico, Turin.
    Museo del Commune, Milan.
    Naples Museum.

Norway: Norsk Folksmuseum, Oslo.
    Ledaal, Stavanger.

Spain: Musee de Historia de la Ciudad, Barcelona.
    Musee Industrias y Artes Populares de Pueblu Español, Barcelona.
    Museo del Ejercite, Madrid.
    Naval Museum, Madrid.

Sweden: Uppsala Universitete Konsthistoriska Institution.

Switzerland: Landesmuseum, Zurich.

U.K. National Army Museum, London.
    Imperial War Museum, London.
    Tower of London.
    Bethnal Green Museum, London.
    Blenheim Palace, Oxfordshire.
    Woburn Abbey, Bedfordshire.
    Museum of Childhood, Edinburgh.
    Scottish United Services Museum, Edinburgh.
    Curragh Camp Military Museum, Republic of Ireland.

U.S.A. West Point Museum, U.S. Military Academy, New York.
    The United States Naval Museum, Annapolis.
    Smithsonian Museum, Washington.
    Heritage Plantation, Sandwich, Massachusetts.

U.S.S.R.: Artillery Museum, Leningrad.

SOCIETIES AND JOURNALS

Austria: 1683 Gesellschaft der Freunde und Sammler kulturhistorischer Figuren, Hernalserhamptstrasse 24, Vienna XVII. Publication 'Sammlernachrichten'.

Belgium: Société Belge d'Etude de l'Uniforme et du Costume, 365, Avenue du Kouter, Bruxelles 5. Publication 'La Figurine'.

Denmark: Forenningen af Tinfigursamlere og Uniformsinteresserede i Danemark, Carl Bernerdsweg 7, Copenhagen. Publication 'Chaketen'.

France: Société des collectionneurs de Figurines Historiques, 38, Rue de Lubeck, Paris XVI. Publication 'Bulletin'.

Germany: Deutche Gesellschaft der Freunde uns sammler kulturhistorischer Zinnfiguren, 3167 Burgdorf, Hannover, Wallgartenstrasse 26, West Germany. Publication 'Die Zinnfigur'.

Italy: Unione Nazionale collezionisti d'Italia, Via Lattanzio 15a, Rome. Publication 'La Voce del Collezionista'.

Netherlands: Stichting ter bevordering von te teepassing van kulturhistorische tinnen Figuren, Eikrodelaan 48, Amsterdam. Publication 'De Tinnen Tafelronde'.

Spain: Agrupacion de Miniaturistas, Rosellon 285, Barcelona. Publication 'Boletin'.

Sweden: Tennsoldatsforeningen, Fruangsgaten 37, Nykoping. Publication 'Drabanten'.

Switzerland: Mitteilungen der Schweizerischen Gesellschaft der Freunde der Zinnfigur, Halseliweg 17, Zurich. Publication 'Figurina Helvetica'.

PLATES FOR REFERENCE

L'Armée Française, ses Uniformes, son Armament, son Equipement by L. Rousselot, Paris.
Soldats et Uniformes du premier Empire by Dr. F. G. Hourtoulle, Clamart Seine.
Heere der Verganenheit by J. Olmes, Krefeld.
Paint-your-own-cards, by R. North, London.

Index

30 cm figures in latex composition of British Infantry Regiment, 1845. A Drummer of the Line with full marching order.

Both are fitted with large plinths to accommodate a regimental plaque. The shako they are wearing is the double peaked black 'Albert' design with a white over red ball tuft.